WE ARE THE WARDS!

A LEGACY OF FAITH AND FAMILY

JAKI HALL & RONALD D. HENDERSON

WESTBOW
PRESS®
A DIVISION OF THOMAS NELSON
& ZONDERVAN

This book is a work of non-fiction. Unless otherwise noted, the author and the publisher make no explicit guarantees as to the accuracy of the information contained in this book and in some cases, names of people and places have been altered to protect their privacy.

WestBow Press books may be ordered through booksellers or by contacting:

WestBow Press
A Division of Thomas Nelson & Zondervan
1663 Liberty Drive
Bloomington, IN 47403
www.westbowpress.com
1 (866) 928-1240

Because of the dynamic nature of the Internet, any web addresses or links contained in this book may have changed since publication and may no longer be valid. The views expressed in this work are solely those of the author and do not necessarily reflect the views of the publisher, and the publisher hereby disclaims any responsibility for them.

Any people depicted in stock imagery provided by Getty Images are models, and such images are being used for illustrative purposes only. Certain stock imagery © Getty Images.

Scripture quotations taken from the King James Version of the Bible.

ISBN: 978-1-9736-7484-9 (sc)
ISBN: 978-1-9736-7486-3 (hc)
ISBN: 978-1-9736-7485-6 (e)

Library of Congress Control Number: 2019914056

Print information available on the last page.

WestBow Press rev. date: 10/24/2019

CONTENTS

PREFACE

The authors of this publication, Rev. Jaki Hall, granddaughter of Otis Ward, and Dr. Ronald D. Henderson, grandson of Laura Ward, have made every effort to gather and report accurate information about the descendants of our great-grandparents, Madison "Matt" and Ella Duncan Ward. However, the rationales for inaccurate or missing information can be many. The following list is not exhaustive but represents the most obvious reasons:

- Early decennial census information of colored or Negro Americans was often inaccurate (i.e., early censuses of 1900 and 1910 listed Ludie Ward as *female* instead of male).

- Authors could not reach many family members for phone, in-person, or mail interviews.
- Some family members declined to be interviewed.

Of paramount importance for *We Are the Wards!* was the need to provide correctly spelled names and accurate birth and death dates (where possible) of the seven or eight offspring of our ancestors that are the major branches of the Ward family tree. Sources referenced are the United States Census reports for 1880, 1890, 1900, 1910, 1920, 1930, and 1940; Alabama Death Records 1908–1959; Alabama Deaths and Burial Index 1881–1974; and the Alabama County Marriages.

ACKNOWLEDGMENTS

We give all praise and honor to God the Father and to our Lord and Savior Jesus the Christ for the insight to undertake this work. It is by the gift of His Holy Spirit that we had the power and continued passion to see this publication to completion.

We are also grateful to the many, many Ward family members, too numerous to list here, who lovingly and willingly filled out the voluminous interview guide and to our aunts, uncles, cousins, brothers, sisters, sons, and daughters who provided information; made corrections, edits, and insertions; and shared photographs, contact information, souvenir journals, obituaries, and so on along the way.

And to our late cousin Cathy Lavern Stewart, granddaughter of Ludie Ward, how can we ever thank her for her devotion to the details of researching and creating the Ward family tree and for the many, many years she committed to that task? It is a magnificent memorial to our family that blesses us every time we view the deep roots and wide reach of the Ward family tree.[1]

We pray that we have represented our faith and family legacy well and have been *chillin' who done Matt and Ella proud*, delighting in the wisdom of Proverbs 4:10–11, 13:

> *Hear, O my son [daughter], and receive my sayings; and the years of thy life shall be many. I have taught thee in the way of wisdom; I have led thee in right paths.... Take fast hold of instruction; let her not go: keep her; for she is thy life.*[2]

---

[1] The Ward family tree can be accessed on Ancestry.com under the Lloyd and Katie Williams branch of the family.

[2] All scriptural references and Bible verses are from the King James Version (KJV).

INTRODUCTION

Rev. Jaki Hall and Dr. Ronald D. Henderson, authors

In January 2017, we took the first steps toward creating a documented, written history of our family, which we have titled *We Are the Wards!* taken from the family anthem written by our cousin Gloria Ward Wyatt, granddaughter of Golden Ward. It is a necessary and substantial complement to the extensive family tree that another cousin, Cathy Lavern Stewart (March 15, 1956–June 17, 2019), created in 2013 with the names of more than seventeen hundred family members and over twelve hundred photographs spread along the various branches. To accompany her herculean effort, we determined to write a factual narrative, as best we could, from data in United States Census reports, official marriage licenses, death certificates, and even obituaries. For the anecdotal history, we interviewed as many of the Wards as we could and mailed lengthy interview guides to family members across the country. Then, we collated the responses to capture ancestral details, special relationships, and familial anecdotes of the loving, proud descendants of Matt and Ella Ward. We knew then that we had to complete this phase of the work—this labor of love—before we lost another generation of elders and, therefore, the precious oral history of our family.

This publication is by no means complete nor is

it always as accurate as we want it to be, but it is a good beginning because of the exceptional support we received from everyone. Perhaps in the years to come, a new family history committee will rise up and tell the rest of the story for the sake of untold Ward generations.

Our prayer is that this volume will commemorate our ancestors, descendants, and heritage with honor as a memorial stone for our children and our children's children so they will know from *whence we have come.*

Additionally, as a continual memorial to our ancestors, we are proposing the establishment of The Matt and Ella Duncan Ward Legacy Scholarship to be awarded during each family reunion to a relative who exemplifies high moral character, community engagement, and academic excellence and who demonstrates a genuine pursuit of higher education. All proceeds from *We Are the Wards!* and contributions will go toward underwriting this fund to continue the family legacy.

CHAPTER 1

A TRIBUTE TO HURVIE MAE STARKS CROWELL

The Ward family reunion, which began forty years ago, is a notable achievement that should not be taken lightly. All the committee members and host cities over the years should be saluted for their diligence and

dedication. A special thank you goes to our elders, now deceased, who strongly supported our reunions in the early years. In addition, it is especially appropriate to commemorate the visionary and initiator of these bi-annual gatherings. Hurvie Mae Starks Crowell. What led her to undertake this herculean feat so long ago? Sister Sharon Starks believes that Hurvie decided to plan the reunions because of the death and home-going service of cousin Melvin Lee Kirkland (great-grandson of Matt and Ella and son of Mary Ella Childs Kirkland) in October 1977. Many family members attended, including Scottie Ward Davis; her late husband, Gus; and their sons, Derwin (now deceased) and Kelvin from Cleveland. There was also a large turnout of relatives from the Detroit area. Shortly afterward, Hurvie stated that our family should not just gather to mourn loved ones in death but should also gather to celebrate loved ones in life.

Others believe she got the idea during one of her trips to Alabama and conversations with cousin Violet (Bie) Ward Cooke. Because Hurvie was asthmatic and could not run and play with the other children, she often sat and talked with grown-ups, or the elders. She also spent a lot of time in deep reflection. Her essay titled "That Old Dusty Dirt Road" is clear evidence of her worldview.

Family funerals, trips to Alabama, and the reflection essay were all factors, even though we cannot with 100 percent certainty identify the catalyst. However, we do believe Hurvie's time spent in Alabama was pivotal. She traveled to Birmingham, Ensley, Fairfield, Bessemer, Uniontown, and finally to Browns, where the Ward story began. In addition to spending time with Violet, she visited with Ed and Bernice Ward, John and Annie Mae Ward, and Hardie Lee and Minnie Ward—all in the family compound—to learn as much as possible about our family.

The question Hurvie asked of her cousin speaks volumes about her enthusiasm to learn the family history: "Bie, will you tell me everything you know about the Ward family?" Bie turned, looked at Hurvie with a smile, and said, "Well, Hurvie Mae, my memory doesn't serve me very well anymore. But of the things I can recall, I remember Grandpa Matt and Grandma Ella being meager farmers and starting out with only the tin-top wooden shanty and a mere acre of land."

That provocative question and, of course, the arresting answer are clear testimony of our cousin's thirst for information about the Wards. But how this knowledge spread beyond Browns to Detroit and to cities all over the country forty years later can only be explained because God's grace inspired a small, Spirit-filled group of family members to catch the vision.

The first reunion took place during the weekend of August 4–6, 1978, at Highlander Inn in Highland Park, Michigan. It was called the Ward/Childs Family Reunion to honor Hurvie's great-grandparents, Madison and Ella Ward, and her maternal grandparents, Laura Ward Childs and Herbert Childs. Documentation of her zeal to create something special can be gleaned from the opening paragraphs of her essay "That Old Dusty Dirt Road."

It has taken much work to put Reunion 1979 together. I began working on this year's reunion last year in August, just two short weeks after the closing of Reunion 1978. In putting Reunion 1979 together, it ultimately carried me to the state of Alabama.

Until her death in 1989, Hurvie was the pied piper of Ward family reunions. She was integral to the development of family directories and the creation of reunion themes. As a result of her efforts, forty years later, we continue to celebrate our heritage and

4

strengthen family ties by gathering every two years in cities across America.

THE ROLL CALL OF REUNIONS

1978: Highland Park, Michigan: "That Old Dusty Dirt Road"

1979: Detroit, Michigan: "Reunion 1979"

1983: Birmingham, Alabama: "Sanders/Ward '83 Reunion: Celebrating Homecoming".

1984: Birmingham, Alabama: "A Family Reunited in Love, Peace, and Prayer"

1986: Detroit, Michigan: "The Year of the Family"

1988: Oakland, California: "We Touch the Future"

1990: Lanham, Maryland/Washington, DC: "The Next Decade: Reflection and Vision"

1992: Cincinnati, Ohio: "All around the Ward"

1994: Birmingham, Alabama: "I Press toward the Mark of the High Calling of God in Christ Jesus"

1996: Detroit, Michigan: "The Heart of the Matter: The Beat Goes On"

1998: Atlanta, Georgia: "Wards Are Celebrating with a Touch of Class"

2000: Cleveland, Ohio: "Just Like Home"

2002: Oakland, California: "Family Is the Tie That Binds"

2004: Baltimore/Washington, DC: "On-WARD! Up-WARD! Sharing a Family Adventure"

2006: Selma, Alabama: "Ward Family Reunion at 'Home'"

2008: Cincinnati, Ohio: "Rich in History, Living in Unity"

2010: Detroit, Michigan: "Ward Family Reunion: 32 Years ... and Counting"

2012: Houston, Texas: "Embarking upon a New Frontier"

2014: Cleveland, Ohio: "Celebrating Our Heritage and Building Our Future"

2016: Birmingham, Alabama: "Ain't No Place Like Home; Ain't Nothing Like Family"

2018: Detroit, Michigan: "The Legacy Continues, 40 Years and Counting"

2020: Atlanta, Georgia:

CHAPTER 2

WHO ARE THE WARDS?

Throughout this historic document, we have repeatedly declared "We Are the Wards!" And at the end of this narrative, we have identified at least four overarching or recurrent themes that distinguish our family.

I. ACTIVE IN AMERICA'S GREAT MIGRATION

(1910–1970s): During the early to mid-twentieth century, the descendants of Matt and Ella were a part of the exodus of millions of African Americans from the South to the North, Midwest, and West in search of economic opportunities and freedom from oppression that ran rampant in Jim Crow country. In the words of acclaimed author Richard Wright of the Harlem Renaissance:

> *I was leaving the south to fling myself into the unknown ... I was taking a part of the South to transplant in alien soil, to see if it could grow differently, if it could drink new and cool rains, bend in strange winds, respond to the warmth of other suns and, perhaps, to bloom.*[3]

Similarly, many Ward family members left the Black Belt of Perry and Dallas Counties in Alabama as part of that great migration to relocate to strange lands miles and miles away to build new lives. Their ability to transplant from the rural, agricultural South to a diverse, industrialized North often added the value of jobs with union contracts offering larger incomes. Family members like Thomas Jefferson Ward, his sister Arlene Ward Shears, Mary Ella Childs Kirkland, members of the Nelson branch of

---

[3] Richard Wright, *Black Boy* (Chicago: Harper and Brothers Publishers, 1945).

the family, siblings of Carrie Jefferson Ward, and so many others migrated to Ohio, Indiana, and Michigan and beyond to Oklahoma and California, making life decisions with historic implications.

II. DEDICATED TO UPWARD MOBILITY

In addition to increased economic opportunities, a strong argument can be made that the greatest impact of our family's movement outside the South was educational attainment. Although Matt and Ella Ward began as modest farmers with *one acre and one mule*, they did lay a solid foundation of faith and family for their offspring to advance in employment and education. College attendance and graduation by determined Ward family members over several generations have been phenomenal—a trend we owe to our ancestors who did not have the opportunity for formal education but valued the importance of it.

Matriculation has occurred at over seventy five institutions of higher learning throughout the nation and the world. Inter-generational changes in occupations have expanded exponentially, from farming to a myriad of professional and entrepreneurial pursuits.

However, the consequence of the great success of this family—which may be a caveat for many other Black families—is that four generations later and beyond, many of Matt and Ella's descendants do not have extensive knowledge or understanding of or an appreciation for their rich family history. Some family members have never been to the homestead in Browns or worshipped at Woodlawn Missionary Baptist Church or even visited the state of Alabama, where their roots run deep. That reality is now clear. Our journey from this humble beginning to residing primarily in states outside of the South, with occupations never imagined by our forebears and in highly successful entrepreneurial endeavors, is the Ward family saga that all family members should know. We must know it in order to tell the generations that follow … lest we forget.

The authors of *We Are the Wards!* pray that the story of the Ward family will begin to answer previously unanswered questions about family members and put faces and formal names to nicknames we only heard in conversations (sometimes whispered in our presence). This book is the first step in moving the Ward family narrative from oral to concrete facts.

III. PASSIONATE ABOUT ENTREPRENEURSHIP

This book would be incomplete without pointing out the capitalistic ethos that took root in early twentieth-century Browns, Alabama. The pioneering steps and ultimate business successes of Otis, Clark Sr., Clark Jr., Hardie Lee, and John Ward, among others, are a testament to their acumen and mastery of navigating in a segregated society with many obstacles for Black entrepreneurs. Yet they prospered, initially with limited options to explore business opportunities within the larger, dominant society. Over time their astute awareness of their *place* and how to interact with white males in buying equipment and other necessities and in selling their produce and products expanded their own commercial successes within the Southern context. Instinctively they knew, as did Matt Ward earlier, that wealth building for the generations to come would begin with land ownership and later with entrepreneurship. In fact, with a close reading, it is apparent that our ancestors explored multiple streams of income at the same time.

Today, opportunities for African Americans are very different, but some of the principles practiced by the Wards more than a hundred years ago are still valuable—belief in God, hard work, ethical dealings, knowledge of the business environment and sound business principles, and the ability to work productively with others, no matter the race.

Below is a sampling of the Ward family members with an American entrepreneurial spirit.

- Rev. Otis (O.D.) Ward owned more than four hundred acres of land that he wanted to keep in the family forever. He also owned a gas station and a country store for which he bought cheese, crackers, and meats in bulk to sell to other Negro families who could not afford to buy these items themselves.

- Clark Edward (Jake) Ward Sr. was a business-farmer who sold milk from the cows he raised to the Uniontown Creamery. He was also able to hire many others, affording them a livelihood, when they worked in his fields during the planting and harvesting seasons. Uncle Jake was known as the Cotton King because, for years, he was the farmer, colored or white, who ginned the first bale of cotton each year.

- Clark Edward (Ed) Ward Jr. was a consummate entrepreneur with a passion for farming, growing soybeans, okra, and cotton, as well as raising cows. He worked with other farmers, assisting, harvesting, and transporting soybeans, hay, and watermelons to market. As owner of the Ward Farms, Ed was the first Black farmer to sell okra to grocery store warehouses in Birmingham, namely Bruno's Warehouse and Food World, and to the farmers market and other privately owned producers. Among his other accomplishments, Ed was the first Black man to own a Black Angus bull.

- Sylvester (Ves) Ward owned and operated the Ward Paint and Body Shop in Uniontown; the business specialized in buying, repairing, and repainting wrecked cars for resale. Ves ran the business for years until a tragic accident at the body shop resulted in his death in 1973.

- Tommy Lincoln Ward and brother Eddie took over the Ward Paint and Body Shop after the death of Ves.

- Hardie Lee Ward, while his father Jake was known as the Cotton King, was called the Okra King because he was so successful in selling okra to stores and food warehouses in Birmingham, Montgomery, and Tuscaloosa, Alabama. During the farming season, Lee would hire up to two hundred workers as graders, pickers, field walkers, record keepers, and truck drivers. From 1987 to 2002, he also owned Ward Auto Sales, a used car and truck dealership where he sold vehicles to neighbors and friends.

- Pastor John Lee Ward, in the Ward tradition, was a farmer with one of the most successful farms in Alabama, owning or leasing nearly fifteen hundred acres of land with a workforce of ten employees. He ran his farm like a corporation by maintaining best business practices and purchasing the biggest John Deere tractors and combines that were manufactured, many of which had air conditioning and radios.

During the latter part of the twentieth century and the early twenty-first centuries, the entrepreneurial spirit is alive and well in Ward descendants. Here are just a few areas of endeavors: real estate, education consulting, cosmetology, publishing, public relations, technology, trucking, franchise ownership, telemarketing, law, and mortuary science.

- Carl Lee Shears was the owner of Nu Classics Publisher, which published scientific articles by researchers, scientists, educators, and futurists in the Washington, DC area. He himself authored fifteen books, among them *Countdown* to *Black Genocide,* and wrote a screenplay titled *Sweet Jesus, Preacher Man.* Carl also published countless scientific essays under the pen name of Saggitarus (*sic*).

- Rev. Jaki Shears Hall was founder and CEO of Jaki Hall Enterprises Inc. (JHE), a public relations and advertising firm. Jaki represented many of Maryland's leading personalities and businesses in creating image campaigns and producing radio and television commercials. JHE also published *The Black Pages* and *Trés Chic Magazine,* a publication for women with a French zest for life.

- Eugene (Gene) Ward, the son of William Ward, owned and operated a coal yard in the mid-sixties.

- Paul Nelson Jr. owns P&P One Care, a carpet-cleaning and handyman service. He is also a franchisee of two companies in Phoenix, Arizona: Coffee News and U-Haul.

- Dr. Terry (Moon) Nelson is founder and CEO of New Generation Education Solutions, LLC, a full-service consulting firm dedicated to improving teaching, learning, and developing programs to increase equity, access, and excellence in education.

- Pastor Phillip White, along with his wife Carla White, owns the Phillip White's Julia L. White Funeral Home in Uniontown. Established in 1874, it is a family-owned, full-service facility that offers, among other services, grief counseling, preplanning services, cremation services, cemetery plots, and a florist shop on the premises.

- Tharone Lee Ward owns and operates Runner Up Trucking, a truck-driving business.

- Andre Ski Taylor has his own T-shirt design business known as Congratulations.

- Dr. Wanda Ward Humphrey is co-founder of Social Media Solutions, LLC. She is a published author, with her latest work called *Help! Drowning in Social Media,* a workbook for P–16 students that addresses social media etiquette, distracted driving, sexting, cyberbullying, loss of academically engaged time, and other perils of misusing technology.

- Jonathon (Joe) Ward and wife Dr. Davida Manor Ward opened two emergency care centers in El Paso, Texas, which they later sold. Joe also owns and operates J/K's Automart, which buys and sells used cars and trucks. His third venture is J's Home Repair, a contracting service providing home and commercial improvement with a specialty in granite installation.

- Mary Turnley, who is multitalented and creative, has established an event-planning consulting business called 2Entertain U, LLC.

- Jeffrey Owen Zeigler is founder of the Ultimate Source, a technology company that offers tech services to government agencies and private clients in the Washington, DC area. He is a software expert who has several software certificates and licenses.

- Jason Omar Zeigler founded RB5 Investments, LLC, which provides homes for homeless veterans. He also established his own law firm, Zeigler Law, LLC, which specializes in real estate law.

- Shana Roianne Hall Graves is the owner of Soma Triune, an executive leadership counseling and training firm designed to elevate the total person: mind, body, and spirit.

- Jalyan Ward owns a full-service beauty salon called Slayed by J. Jalyan specializes in providing hair weave and wig services to women in the Houston area.

- Kalyan has entered the beauty field and started a successful eyelash business in Houston, Texas.

Finally, there is no equivocation that the seeds of self-employment planted in the Black Belt of Alabama continue to grow within the descendants of Matt and Ella Ward throughout the United States.

IV. FAITHFUL TO GOD

However, most important and foundational to the Ward family—and what has sustained us over the centuries—has been our enduring faith in God, emphatically declaring that He is the Creator and Sustainer of all life and that nothing happens without His permissive will. We believe that Jesus Christ is the only begotten Son of the Father, sent to save us from our sins—that He was born of a virgin, was crucified on the cross at Calvary, died, was buried, and was raised early on the third day with all power in His hands. And because He lives, our family can face each tomorrow with faith.

We were taught about the grace and mercy of

Almighty God to encourage our hearts during difficult days. For centuries, Matt and Ella's offspring have taken to heart the words of Paul in Philippians 4:19, when he said, "But my God shall supply all your need according to his riches in glory by Christ Jesus." Our God has met our every need, from that meager farm and shack in Browns to our cousin John operating an agribusiness and owning over fifteen hundred acres and cousin Ed hiring more than two hundred workers at the height of his farming career. The Ward family has been and still is blessed and highly favored of God!

Our Christian faith has been the bedrock of our very existence for nearly two hundred years. Our forebears left a faith legacy that has continued to the fourth and fifth generations and beyond. It is borne out in the way we strive to live moral, principled lives every day and in the numbers of pastors, ministers, evangelists, prophets, elders, and other propagators of the gospel of Jesus Christ, our Lord and Savior. The early family focus on Woodlawn Missionary Baptist Church and Trinity Baptist Church, where the late Rev. Otis Ward, the eldest child of Matt and Ella, pastored for years, should not be overlooked. Generations later, the following family members continue to carry out that legacy and the three T's of our Christian faith: time, talent, and treasure. What follows is a partial list of the Ward descendants who have been called into ministry, along with faith statements by several others.

Pastor Otis (O.D.) Ward, the oldest of Matt and Ella's children, pastored the Woodlawn Missionary Baptist Church and Trinity Baptist Church in Browns, Alabama.

Rev. Ludie Ward, one of the seven or eight children of Matt and Ella, established a home church in Ensley, Alabama.

Pastor John Lee Ward, grandson of Rev. Otis (O. D.) Ward, is our elder statesman! At eighty-three years old, he is the oldest living minister in our family and, without doubt, the longest preaching member. And if the truth be told, he began practicing preaching as a child and then later as a young man before he was even licensed to traffic in the Word of God.

During his early years whenever a cat or dog died, John would *preach* the funeral. Devoid of a robe or pulpit, he just stood near the animal and pretended to be a preacher to lay it to rest. Family who happened to be around gathered at the would-be burial site to attend the funeral service, listening to John preach the eulogy and perform the committal service. At that time, John had no idea what the Lord had in store for him.

When John was a teenager, according to his sister Dot, he would walk around their home in Browns practicing his favorite sermon, "The Eagle Stirs Her Nest," taken from Deuteronomy 32: 11–12:

> *As an eagle stirreth up her nest, fluttereth over her young, spreadeth abroad her wings, taketh them, beareth them on her wings: So the Lord alone did lead him, and there was no strange god with him.*

Providentially, the Spirit of Almighty God had been stirring in John's heart for decades, and although he knew there was a great calling on his life, he resisted it for years. Finally, one day as he was walking from his home to his farm shop, he heard screaming from the sweltering heat and flames resulting from an explosion at the Ward Paint and Body Shop owned by his nephew Sylvester (Ves) Ward.

With no regard for his own life, John opened the side door to the body shop and rescued his nephews Sylvester and Eddie from the inferno. As a result of the fire, John's left hand was severely burned, and an area on the right side of his face was slightly burned. The family doctor, Dr. Deramus, treated his burns for a very long time after he was discharged from the hospital. During the many visits, Dr. Deramus had to scrape the flesh from John's hand to ensure that it would heal properly. Wanda, his daughter who was just four years old at that time, helped nurse him back to health by making a schedule to administer his medicine after his wife, Annie Mae, returned to her job as an elementary school teacher.

This was the turning point. A short time later, John Lee Ward accepted God's call to preach the Gospel of Jesus Christ. The Saturday he accepted his call, his wife and daughter were surprised to see more than the usual number of cars in their driveway when they returned home from Selma. As they approached the house, John bolted out the door, saying, "I got to preach!" Annie Mae replied, "Well, go on and preach. If you have to preach, preach."

In the fullness of time, this successful farmer became a *fisher of men*, as Jesus declared to His disciples in Matthew 4:19, "Follow me, and I will make you fishers of men." He went from farming in the pastures of Browns, Alabama, to pastoring several churches in Dallas County and presently pastoring two churches: Antioch Missionary Baptist Church (the first church he was called to pastor) for the past forty-six years and Good Hope Missionary Baptist Church for thirty-six years in Orrville and Sardis, Alabama, respectively. Under his leadership, significant growth has taken place. Among the most notable accomplishments is the construction of new edifices at both churches. Rev. Ward accepts pastoral duties with humility; he visits the sick even when they are hospitalized over one hundred miles from his home, counsels the brokenhearted, and baptizes those who accept Jesus Christ as their Savior. In addition, he attends celebrations, officiates at weddings between a man and a woman, and reminds young people every Sunday to "stay focused."

When asked about what convinced him long ago that the hand of God was on his life and that he was indeed called to ministry, the Rev. John Lee Ward answered succinctly, "You just know."

Rev. Willie James Paige was the son of Lincoln (Buddy) Ward and grandson of Rev. Otis (O.D.) Ward. Rev. Paige was a minister in Cleveland, Ohio.

Rev. Jaki Hall, granddaughter of Rev. Otis (O. D.) Ward

My Father told me to tell you that
everything is going to be all right.

I saw a figure draped in white, standing with outstretched arms and a halo of blazing sunlight outlining his form. His voice was clear, warm, and welcoming. It was as if I were talking with someone in my bedroom as I lay staring out the open window. But I was alone in that room on Sea Shadow Place with no one in sight, in fact, with no one else in the house.

The light from the silhouette pierced my soul. I had never experienced anything like it before and did not understand the image, the words, or the sudden peace I felt because it was the worst, most depressing time of my life: my marriage had ended, my television show was canceled, my business had collapsed, my health had failed, and my home was in foreclosure. How could I have peace when I was at the end of my rope, preparing to move from a nine-room house in prestigious Columbia, Maryland, to one room with my sister Doll?

But, somehow deep in my soul, I knew it was Jesus sent by God to come see about me. And I took Him at His word. This "party girl," dressed to the nines, dancing and drinking all night, making every Friday night happy hour at one of her favorite night spots in the tri-state area, had played out. However, I knew *that everything was going to be all right,* even though I didn't know how; even worse, I didn't have the energy to consider how. I simply rested in Jesus, who had come to this *prodigal daughter* in her darkest hour.

That was the beginning of my new life in Christ, when I surrendered my all—just like I did in the world. First, I had to find a Bible-believing, Bible-teaching church where my daughter Shana and I could worship. God, in His infinite wisdom, led us to the right church at the right time—the New Shiloh Baptist Church in Baltimore where the late prophetic preacher Dr. Harold A. Carter Sr. was the pastor. A protégé of slain civil rights icon Dr. Martin Luther King Jr., Pastor Carter was a fireball preacher who sounded much like his mentor, melding theological scholarship and

Black liberation theology with a down-home, Selma, Alabama, tenor that thrust the worshippers into the throne room of God every service. His intellect, racial pride, and Southern bent spoke to my spirit to transport me back to my grandfather's little church in Browns.

Next I enrolled Shana and myself in New Shiloh's Saturday Church School for Bible study. I remember my first lesson was from John 14, and my first memory verse was 18, when Jesus was preparing His disciples for His departure and said, "I will not leave you comfortless; I will come to you." It immediately became my life's focus because it confirmed my experience years before in my bedroom and encouraged me to hold on a little while longer. Sha and I did just that and became involved in as many church activities as possible. As I grew in grace in the things of God, Pastor Carter appointed me co-leader of the Stewards of Christ, a group of disciples in training. He later ordained me as a deacon in what he called *the greatest church God has anywhere.*

It was my turning point; I decided to follow Jesus Christ, to live for Him with the same passion I had spent serving and celebrating the world. It was during this time that I received the call to ministry, to preach the gospel of Jesus Christ to the lost, the lonely, the left-out, the least of these. For nearly eight years, however, I ran from the call, exclaiming that I needed assurance it was from God and not wishful thinking on my part. In retrospect, I'm not certain what would have convinced me that it was indeed a divine assignment from my heavenly Father, but I waited and waited, running and running. Then, one Saturday afternoon, a saint of the Lord, Deacon Vera James, pulled me aside to admonish me, saying, "God has told me to tell you that there is a call on your life and if you don't answer it, He will take the mantle from you and give it to someone else." Before she could finish, I began weeping like a baby, knowing the time had come; I could run no more. (Prophetically, this was the second messenger sent by God to me.)

In 2004, I preached my initial sermon titled "Broken but Blessed," declaring how God had taken the fragments of my life to bless me, despite it all. I also preached how God had been there all along, even during the nightclub days when I twirled all night long on the dance floors of the world. Now, I only dance for Jesus.

To prepare for ministry, I enrolled in the Ecumenical Institute of St. Mary's Seminary and University to earn a master's of theology; began teaching in New Shiloh's Saturday Church School, the school that had once nurtured my soul and my daughter's; and joined the faculty of the Determined Biblical and Theological Institute. I also started an outreach ministry called The Daughters of Dorcas, Inc., a Christian nonprofit that has adopted two orphanages in Port-au-Prince, Haiti. The outreach ministry also funds programs for at-risk male teens, feeds the hungry, clothes the naked, visits the sick and shut-ins, and witnesses Christ to lost souls. This group of ten saintly women raises funds every year to give away, but more importantly, we give ourselves away in service—all to the glory of God.

This is my new life in Christ! And I want only to live for Jesus in the power of the Holy Ghost. In the words of the Apostle Paul in Philippians 3:7–8, 10:

> *But what things were gain to me, those I counted loss for Christ. Yea doubtless, and*

I count all things but loss for the excellency
of the knowledge of Christ Jesus my Lord:
for whom I have suffered the loss of all
things, and do count them but dung, that
I may win Christ. That I may know him,
and the power of His resurrection, and the
fellowship of His sufferings, being made
conformable unto his death.

Pastor Cheryl Diane Taylor Frazier is the great-granddaughter of Rev. Otis (O. D.) Ward. For nearly twenty years, she has served as co-pastor of Beracah Faith Ministries International  in Temecula, California with her husband Apostle Glenn Curtis Frazier Sr. Before relocating to Southern California, Pastor Cheryl and Apostle Frazier planted Gospel Palace Ministries in Cleveland, Ohio, and pastored there for seventeen years. Steeped in the Word of God, Cheryl received her ministry training through the Ashland Theological Seminary special course with certificates from Case Western Reserve University in Cleveland.

She is truly an anointed psalmist and evangelist who has traveled across the United States and across the globe, including England, Canada, South Africa, and the Bahamas. Pastor Cheryl ministers the spoken Word in services, workshops, and conferences throughout the nation, and as she ministers in song, people have been delivered from demon oppression and depression and have received physical healing as the anointing of God flows through her. With the voice of an angel, our cousin recorded a CD in 1990 entitled *Remember,* which contains songs of inspiration and has blessed thousands of people around the world in South Africa, the Bahamas, and Europe. Additionally, she recorded a special project with Arrow Records and a single project with her son Kevin entitled "I'm Broken" that is currently available for download on iTunes. Pastor Cheryl has also appeared on various television ministries, such as with Bishop T. D. Jakes, Dr. Creflo Dollar, and Dr. Rod Parsley, and continues to minister at local churches, both large and small.

Cheryl Frazier is married to Apostle Glenn Curtis

Frazier Sr. Together, they serve as apostolic oversight of Shiloh Christian Ministries of Idyllwild, California; New Life Faith Ministries of Ravenna, Ohio; and Turning Point International Ministries of Ontario, California. They also provide prayer covering for Unity of the Faith Ministries and many others in Southern California and Cleveland, Ohio.

The Fraziers are parents of two fine and gifted sons, Glenn Jr. (Mann) and Kevin, both of whom assisted them in ministry as church musicians in Ohio. They have two daughters-in-law, Tracy and Tomorrow Frazier. Apostle and Cheryl Frazier are also the proud grandparents of six grandchildren and one great-granddaughter.

Evangelist Wendy Ladell Taylor Hairston, great-granddaughter of Rev. Otis (O. D.) Ward, is in ministry with her husband, Evangelist Wendell Hairston, at Beracah Faith Ministries International, the church where her sister Cheryl and brother-in-law are co-pastors.

Pastor Phillip White is the great-great-grandson of Rev. Otis (O. D.) Ward.

Before I answered my call to ministry, I dealt with many issues, especially my love for playing blackjack at the casinos. Once on my way to play, I heard the voice of God say, "Turn the car around and go home and preach." Even after I discussed this with my wife, Carla, I went on to the casino, and that night, I won thousands of dollars. As my winnings grew, another gambler remarked that she had never seen someone so sad while he was winning.

That night Phillip had an epiphany, that even though he was winning, he was actually losing.

In 2000, by the providence of God, our cousin turned his car and his life around to answer the call to ministry. He preached his initial sermon on January 28, 2001. With the title "A Man Called Jesus," Phillip chose John 9:1–3 as his text, one detailing the story of the man who was blind from birth and the disciples inquiring, "Master, who did sin, this man or his parents, that he was born blind?" Jesus answered, "Neither hath this man sinned, nor his parents: but that the works of God should be made manifest in him."

What confirmed to Phillip that he was finally in the will of God occurred on the day he preached what was once called a trial sermon: on that very day the pastor of the church resigned. The moderator then sent our cousin there to lead the small congregation that was without an under-shepherd. Later, he was chosen by the people and installed as pastor of Mount Olive Missionary Baptist Church in Gallion, Alabama. The Olive, as it is affectionately called, is a church devoted to family growth and to God's vision to a blessed people.

Elder Paul Nelson, grandson of Golden Ward, was among the first elders to be consecrated at Azusa World Ministries in 1998.

Elder Donald Nelson, grandson of Golden Ward, became the family's first elder of the Church of Christ in 2017 in Cleveland, Ohio.

Rev. Gloria Ward Wyatt, granddaughter of Golden Ward

A heart passionately seeking the Father is truly in the DNA of Gloria Ward Wyatt. She is a woman on a mission to share, reveal, and make His truth known: "And ye shall know the truth, and the truth shall make you free" (John 8:32). As a minister of God's unconditional love, Gloria teaches the Word, moves in a powerful prophetic anointing, and displays a truly contagious joy of the Lord in her speaking and singing. For twenty-six years, she was one of the lead singers for the contemporary Christian, all-female band known as Frontline, traveling throughout the Midwest to minister at retreats, conventions, churches, and outreach events. She is, in fact, the author of the Ward family anthem, *We Are the Wards.*

Gloria Wyatt was called by God when she was just a little girl at the First Baptist Church in Fairfield, Alabama. She became a young "missionette" with a heart for evangelism and missions. Even at that time, she always knew there was more to her life than just singing in the choir. She is truly a gifted and unleashed worshipper of God.

Gloria has traveled to over thirty states, including Alaska and Hawaii, as well as globally to the nations of Africa; to Germany, Canada, and Mexico; and three times to Israel. Wherever God leads her, she shares the truth of what it means to be sealed with the full knowledge of God in all spiritual wisdom, as the Apostle Paul states in Colossians 1:9, "For this cause we also, since the day we heard it, do not cease to pray for you, and to desire that ye might be filled with the knowledge of his will in all wisdom and spiritual understanding."

Living in Detroit as a young mother, Gloria became involved in helping international students at Wayne State University. This international connection stemmed from her work with the inner-city congregation of Eber Baptist Church. From there, she ministered through street evangelism, feeding the homeless and reaching out to people of all walks of life on Cass Avenue in Detroit.

Gloria was involved in fund-raisers for the Detroit Rescue Mission as they often called upon her as a gifted psalmist. She was sought after for bringing life-changing messages of exhortation for the Women's Division of Detroit Teen Challenge and the youth at the Detroit Impact Center. She was also recruited to sing and teach with the Underground Railroad Church in Windsor, Canada, returning numerous times to bless and encourage the Canadian people.

This powerful woman of God is a true bridge builder, reaching across generations and cultures. Her ministry and partnership with the Native American people is a testimony of her ability to connect people of every tongue, tribe, and nation.

Providentially, in 1983, God led Gloria Ward Wyatt to become involved in Women's Aglow, which opened doors to numerous speaking and singing engagements. Later, this international women's ministry transitioned to include men and became known as Aglow International. Continuing to serve for over thirty-five years, Gloria served as hostess, worship leader, secretary, local president, area board leader, and presently as leader of the Michigan Southeast Region as area president.

She is one of the founders of the long-standing

Michigan Capital Prayer Team, traveling to Lansing, Michigan, for over twenty-seven years to impact the state governmental structure through the power of prayer. She continues to be part of a powerful network of prayer warriors changing and influencing the course of local, state, and national judicial and legislative government.

Her ministerial training includes certifications from the School of Evangelism of Eber Baptist Church and the Detroit Ministers Association, where she completed the School of Ministry program in 2008. She also completed the School of Prophetic Training in her state. After years of preparation, she gained entrance to the state prisons in Michigan through the coursework and certification under Chuck Colson's ministry.

A faithful, unwavering servant, she is a true vessel of God's joy. It is often shared that this woman of the Highest God has you laughing one minute and crying the next, and all the while, she reveals truths that change your life forever: This is the Reverend Gloria Ward Wyatt.

Pastor Eric West Nelson, the great-grandson of Golden Ward, pastors the United in Christ Ministries Church in Bakersfield, California.

Rev. Leon B. Morehead, great-grandson of Golden Ward

The Call I Didn't Want to Answer

As a child I knew something was different about me. I enjoyed wearing suits and playing "church" more than anything else. I couldn't understand why I would enjoy the moment of  "playing" the role of the preacher so much instead of being the soloist or choir director or anything else. I always felt it was because as much as my mom had us in church, I thought we should have gotten our mail and phone calls there. Reality is, there was a call on my life that I knew about as a child but wanted to do everything possible not to be ridiculed as *the church boy*. See, I remember vividly in elementary school how those who openly discussed how much they went to church were the easiest prey and wearing glasses and having the last name of Morehead gave me two strikes, and I definitely didn't want the third strike by being a church boy.

This led to a long-term pattern of toeing the fine line of mischievous and rebellious behavior because I had to prove the point that I was a normal person who didn't want to be set apart to speak in season and out of season what the Lord would want shared. I looked at the call to preach the Gospel as a heartache, not to help heal hearts.

When I turned seventeen, I was a senior in high school and basically was told that I wouldn't be able to run much longer. So instead of accepting that call to ministry then, I promised the Lord that I would help with the youth of the church in any way He saw fit. I worked summer camp and vacation Bible school, then transitioned after high school to teaching church school and Bible study, coaching basketball, and doing anything else that I thought would give God the glory without my having to be a preacher. While the call became louder in various forms, I tried to dull the call with anything I thought would allow me to stay in the pew and not in the pulpit. Of course, I was a fool who refused to realize that no matter how much I negotiate with God, He will always get what He wants, and I would give Him what He wanted in due time.

I should have known that all my negotiating to work in different areas of ministry was a period of preparation that trained me to be the youth minister and then elevate me to executive minister, which means full-time ministry that includes all the duties I had done during my negotiating period and more.

My journey isn't for everybody because I am a better servant for everybody to know that I'm a nobody trying to tell everybody about Somebody who can save anybody.

(Rev. Leon's joy of the Lord and his sense of humor precede him. Most of the time, he can be found in a jovial and giving mood. He credits his giving personality as an inheritance from his mother, Mrs. Geraldine Rutledge Johnson, granddaughter of Golden Ward.)

Elder Mary Helen Kirkland Dixson, granddaughter of Laura Ward

I cannot say when I was called into ministry because I had been in church most of my life. But in 1997, I began to develop a relationship with God, and I stopped simply being a *churchgoer* and came  into a relationship with God through the study of His Word. I began to understand that knowing God was to know and do His will. Starting at home was my first ministry. My children were brought up in the church, but they learned to establish their own relationships with God just as I was learning.

I began a women's ministry outside of the church I attended at that time—Word of Faith International Christian Center (WOFICC). The ministry was approved after I sent information to Bishop Keith Butler, who became my overseer, regarding the vision and mission of Sisters United for Christ, a group of faithful women who ministered to other women from various backgrounds and denominations. We began clothing those who were coming out of a rehab facility called Genesis House, feeding them naturally as well as spiritually during our fellowships in the community room of my development at the time. Many women were blessed and received Christ as their Lord and Savior. Standards were set for the women who worked with us as we all attempted to live more Christ-like, according to His Word. This fellowship grew and lasted for over ten years. After the group disbanded, many of the women went on to start other ministries under their respective churches as God called them to do.

During this time, I completed a two-year study of the Bible at WOFICC and graduated from the class. I was honored that my mother, Mary Ella Childs Kirkland, was able to attend the graduation, along with my children, grandchildren, and sisters who were members of our group. In 2009, I began to fellowship with Tabernacle of Faith International, where I worked alongside my husband, Pastor Bishop Danny Dixson Sr., who acknowledged the teaching call on my life. I was ordained as an elder a year later by my husband's best friend, Pastor Claudette Clark. I continue to work and serve wherever I am needed in ministry.

Today, I recognize that being a minister does not mean being served but serving. I enjoy the nurturing aspect of my life as a woman of God, being a mother to many as well as to my own children and grandchildren. Also, I enjoy mentoring others and taking on administrative assignments to organize and discern the gifts of others in order to nurture those gifts. I look forward to other venues that God will call me to naturally as well as spiritually. At this point in my life, I know where I am and who I am in Christ.

I thank God for His appointments for me, and I look forward to my future walk as I make myself available for His use.

> *Though I speak with the tongue of men and angels, and have not charity [love for others growing out of God's love for me], I am become as sounding brass, or tinkling cymbal [just an annoying distraction].*
> *1 Corinthians 13:1 (with exegetical interpretations)*

Elder Tamara (Micki) Lots, great-granddaughter of Laura Ward

I grew up in a single-parent household where my mother's motto was, "But as for me and my house, we will serve the Lord" (Joshua 24:15). Every Sunday, we went to church and were very active. We did not attend a random church but a non-denominational ministry that my grandparents founded. Going to church and engaging in ministry was very important to me at an early age. During the summer of 1990, when I was fifteen years old, I *kept* having visions of myself speaking before large groups of people. I did not know if that was professional or spiritual. I asked God to show me what it meant. Over the next couple of years, I began to learn how to listen to the voice of God, to pray more, and to be sensitive and attentive as far as my future and purpose for being on this earth. I sensed a strong call of God to *teach*. During my junior year of high school, I made a final decision to go to school to study education. It was then that I accepted my call to the Five-Fold Ministry as a teacher. According to Ephesians 4:11–12, "And he gave some, apostles; and some, prophets; and some evangelists; and some, pastors and teachers; For the perfecting of the saints, for the work of the ministry, for the edifying of the body of Christ." I joined the new ministry class that our church was offering and completed it in four years. At the age of twenty-one, I was consecrated as a teacher at my local assembly and was recognized as a minister.

I delivered my initial sermon when I was seventeen. From the age of nineteen, I was a Sunday School teacher and directed vacation Bible school for ten years. I've taught Bible study and have done everything in ministry that I've been asked to do, was in my power to do, and was God's will for me to do. Since 2002, I've worked with our women's ministry and co-directed with a phenomenal woman of God from 2010 until now. This ministry has allowed me to speak and minister to women and their families. I've been able to lead and facilitate discipleship groups and coordinate events for the growth and fellowship of women. I worked with our youth ministry from 2004 to 2007, then began directing Christian education from 2007 to 2010.

In 2012, I was officially ordained as an evangelist and, in 2013, an elder. In the last two years, I was appointed as lead elder, meaning I was able to assist my father with various leadership roles. He is training me as a pastor as his task is to "lead for the future."

My life has been ministry, and I have no regrets. I love to serve, teach, and counsel people. I am curious to see what God is about to do with me regarding ministry. My son is about to leave for college, meaning both of my children will be gone at the same time. As a result, my time will be free to do ministry and live my life.

Finally, I am a third-generation leader of my church ministry. My grandfather knew my father would take over the ministry (even when he was a prodigal son, still in the streets). My grandmother pastored the church and stood in the gap for twelve years until my dad took over the ministry. Just as my grandmother "held the ministry together" until my father walked into his role, I will probably stand in the gap until my son walks into his role. My father's vision is for his grandson, my son Ky-Lee, to take over the ministry— our family legacy.

My desire is not to just "have church" but for us to do community work. I envision a day care, transportation, and counseling ministry/business. I would like to feed and assist the community with various resources. I would like for us to be a resource agency where we are taking care of the local church body, as well as helping the city of Highland Park, Michigan, and its surrounding communities.

CHAPTER 3

A FAMILY DECLARATION

Since the days of Madison "Matt" and Ella Duncan Ward, our family, out of a long-standing Baptist tradition, has covenanted with Almighty God that He will save our family and that all the generations to come will serve Jesus Christ our Lord with gladness. We also declare, according to the promises of God and on the prayers of our ancestors, that He will bless our households and heal the land.

This we declare in agreement with Acts 2:39 in scripture that "For the promise is unto you, and to your children, and to all that are afar off, even as many as the Lord our God shall call." The Bible teaches in Revelation 5:8 that prayers are eternal, that they are kept in heaven and presented before the altar with golden censers with the prayers of the saints. So the descendants of Matt and Ella stake our households as symbols of our faith—covering our family with the blood of Jesus Christ and lifting the prayers of our ancestors, declaring that the children's children to the millennial generation shall be saved.

The strength of our family and of most Black families since slavery has been critical to each member's surviving the degradation of that inhumane system, post-Reconstruction, the Black codes, Jim Crowism, and institutional racism. In the African-American culture, we continue to depend on the support of our nuclear and extended families as the source of help and survival. Centuries ago, and even now, the Wards vowed not to allow those heinous systems working against our people break our spirits or our familial bond. Even today, we strongly believe in family, although we know each generation will be bombarded with new challenges, new values, and new lifestyles. However, the elders are challenged to be great role models, setting high standards for each generation to follow. We are also called to pray without ceasing that as our sons and daughters adapt to emerging trends, they will not compromise the Christian values taught long ago.

CHAPTER 4
UNIONTOWN, ALABAMA

Uniontown, Alabama, is essential to our story because it is just eight miles from where Matt and Ella established the Ward family homestead. According to the official website of the City of Uniontown, it was initially called Woodville, which was founded in 1818 and incorporated nearly twenty years later.[4] Located in southwestern Perry County in the west-central part of the state, Woodville, by 1860, had grown to support educational facilities for boys and girls. As with all segregated schools in the South, most colored children in the community attended Perry County Training School (now the Robert C. Hatch High School). Several of our family members remember the all-Negro faculty and student body. And even

---

[4] The history of Uniontown can be found at Uniontown.org/history.html.

though many of the Wards attended school locally, others traveled to Marion to matriculate at Lincoln High School, a private boarding institution.

Uniontown also had several businesses on Main Street, but its economy was driven by the burgeoning cotton crops on the surrounding plantations because of the fertile black topsoil in the state. Known as the Black Belt region of the South, including Alabama, the area later took on a dual meaning when most farmworkers were former slaves who, when freed, stayed local as either sharecroppers or tenant farmers, becoming the county's majority population.

Historically, the town became known as Uniontown in 1861 and remained an agricultural economy after the Civil War. In 1897, the Uniontown Cotton Oil Company was established as one of the first facilities of its kind in the state, manufacturing cottonseed oil and cotton seed meal. By 1900, the town had cotton gins, cotton warehouses, and a cotton mill. However, in less than two decades, the town lost population as more people moved off plantations to escape oppression and because of the devastation caused by the boll weevil (beetle) that fed on the cotton crop. Infesting cotton buds, the boll weevil caused a nearly 50 percent decline in the cotton crop. This devastation changed not only the economy of the region but also the complexion of Uniontown.

Cousin Dorothy (Dot) Ward Reeves, great-granddaughter of Matt and Ella, recalls that US Highway 80 ran through the Main Street and business section of the little town called Uniontown, and most agreed that if you blinked too long, you would be in and out of the city gate before you opened your eyes. It had two traffic signals, a cotton gin, three department stores, a post office, a movie theater, a drug store, a grocery store, a hardware store, and a furniture store. A man of color, James Furnis, operated a print shop in the main business district. However, most "colored" (during the early years, we were called *colored*) businesses were clustered on one street of the town. That one street included a café, two grocery stores, a shoe-shine stand, and a shoe repair shop. Also located in the immediate area were three funeral homes and beauty parlors that were owned by colored people.

In the farm community, called Hamburg Road/ Dallas Field, there were three colored-owned grocery stores owned by the William Dansby, Abe Young, and Booker Starks families. These stores supplied the basic needs of families until they were able to go into town. The Dansby family also owned a gas station. For entertainment, colored folk had one night club and a baseball team called the Uniontown Black Steers.

Outside of church, Uniontown was the highlight of the week and the center of most family activity for shopping and meeting and greeting friends. Fathers and grandfathers would treat their youngsters to rides, sometimes on top of bales of cotton, into town on Saturdays. According to Ralph Edward Ward Sr., son of Clark Edward Ward and Bernice Jordan Ward, his grandfather Jake took him everywhere with him, including to town where Ralph was given money to buy penny candy and five-cent drinks. Many young people like Ralph would dress up almost like going to church on Sundays, with the boys wearing starched-ironed jeans and "Sunday-go-da-meetin'" dress shirts. Girls, on the other hand, with hair slicked down with old-fashioned pressing combs and greased-down legs, wore crisp skirts and blouses. Teenagers delighted in these weekly excursions by walking up and down the street (often with hope of meeting someone of the opposite sex) from the time they arrived in town with their parents or grandparents until time to go home. Adults used these trips to chat with friends and take care of business.

CHAPTER 5
OUR PATRIARCH AND MATRIARCH

Ella Duncan Ward and grandson Clark Edward Ward Sr.
To family members, Clark closely resembled his grandfather, Matt.

E ight miles from Uniontown, in Browns, Alabama,
Madison "Matt" Ward and Ella Duncan Ward

put down roots in that fertile black soil to establish what became the Ward compound, a cluster of four wood-framed homes located just across the old dusty dirt road from one another. What follows is a detailed historical and anecdotal family history handed down from generation to generation of our forebears, who lived in Alabama in the mid-nineteenth century. According to the 1900 Twelfth Census of the United States, Madison Ward—son of Alonzo Ward and Rachael Ward—was born in Wythe, Virginia, in February 1845 and died in Uniontown on October 1, 1929, at the age of eighty-four. He was one of the nine children (six half-siblings) Alonzo Ward fathered with three different women—Elizabeth Mallett, Rachael Ward, and Hannah Ward, the latter of whom is described in the 1870 Federal Census as the *inferred spouse of Alonzo's inferred children.*

Elizabeth Mallett	Rachael Ward	Hannah Ward
John Marvin Ward	**Madison "Matt" Ward**	Laura Ward (1848)
1881–1952	1845–1929	Liberty Ward (1857)
	Charlotte Ward	James Ward (1857)
	1862–1933	Rhoda Ward
	James Ward	Alexander "Alex" Ward

The US Schedule 1 Population Report (1900) also shows that Matt's parents were Virginia natives, as were Ella's mother and father, Ida and William Duncan. However, Ella was born in Perry County, Alabama, in February 1853. Ella and Matt eventually settled in Dallas County in a community known as Dallas Field.

And even though *colored folks wuz not 'lowed tu marry doin' slavery,* these former slaves were blessed to be issued a marriage license by the State of Alabama on February 19, 1876, and were married soon after.

The official marriage license of Madison and Ella Duncan Ward[5]

5 Ancestry.com, s.v. "Ella Dunkin," https://www.ancestry.com/sharing/ 13781132?h=7ee5da&oxid=61782&olid=61782&o sch=Email+Programs

To this union, seven, possibly eight, children were born: Otis, Isabella (Isabelle), Ludie, William, Golden, Davis, John, and Laura—all of whom lived in their home state until their deaths.

We believe that during slavery, Matt worked as a farmhand or house slave in the main dwelling of his plantation owner. In succeeding years as a freed slave, he likely worked as a sharecropper or tenant farmer, work that often benefited the landowner more than himself. However, his years of hard labor far exceeded his economic resources because many times he barely broke even at harvest time either due to previous debts or miniscule profits. Therefore, at some point, Matt and Ella stood on their faith and turned their eyes toward the future, in agreement with Psalm 121—"lifting up [their] eyes unto the hills, from whence cometh [their] help … [their] help cometh from the Lord, which made heaven and earth"—with a desire that they, too, might become landowners in order to provide an abundant life for their family. They intuitively knew that landownership would confer upon the family a measure of dignity, independence, and financial security. They instinctively knew to give their children proprietary claims to the land like any other man, white or colored. They indisputably knew that owning land was a sign of prosperity and the beginning of inter-generational wealth-building for untold Ward descendants. Dropping their buckets where they were, these newly freed slaves purchased one acre of land with a small wooden shack and called it *home*.

Deeply committed to their faith and family, Matt and Ella worked diligently to build a legacy that stretched beyond that one-acre lot they owned at the beginning of their marriage. On the farm at "the fork in the road in Dallas County," the Wards became successful farmers, primarily growing cotton at that time along with a variety of vegetables, as well as raising cattle. A century later, only one descendant, great-grandson Rev. John Lee Ward (son of Clark and Pearlie Black Ward) had continued to farm, until he retired in 1999 after successfully diversifying his crops to include soybeans, okra, and peanuts.

Grandpa Matt and Grandma Ella raised their children on the farm and, when necessary, took in at least three sets of grandchildren when their parents passed away. These grandchildren included the three children of son Ludie after his wife Rebecca died (Albert, Roberta, and Katie Mae); Isabella's infant daughter Blanche; and Laura's two girls, Mary Ella and Ethel Ruby. To Matt and Ella, family was their greatest asset. Devout Baptists, they instilled Christian and family values in their offspring while impressing upon them the importance of moral character and a strong work ethic.

Dot, sister of John, describes the Ward legacy this way:

> Although we don't all see each other often, there is a special bond among the siblings, nephews, nieces and cousins. In some way or another, we have always shown concern for and rallied around each other. There is a strong sense of value and pride in the family. Even now, I am proud to be a Ward and have taught my two children the value of family, professional work habits, the importance of giving back and helping others. The Ward family name means I have much

to live up to. As a Ward, I learned to put
Christ first in all that I do and to make
Him the center of my being.

These principles have served us well to the third,
fourth, fifth generations and beyond and continue
to this day. The hallmarks of our family are our
Christian faith, our integrity, our solid work ethic, and
our financial stability. In addition, the Wards—young
and old—have always been a caring, compassionate
people.

This is a very loving family that has
stayed close. And now that I am older
(90 years) and look back, I now admire
and appreciate how rich that part of
my life is. The Ward family means the
world to me; I'm so glad we have the
Ward family reunions so that we can
continue to connect with one another,
says Violet Odessa Ward Ridgeway,
great-granddaughter.

Echoing these sentiments, Larry McCall, son of Lucie Cooke McCall Dawson and great-great-grandson of Matt and Ella, says,

> The Wards have always been a loving, kind and proud family, though not without fault. But we love one another and are there for each other because the apple does not fall far from the tree. We live and love. We work and play. We teach and pray.

The impact of our ancestors is deeply felt today, although very little is known about Matt himself because he died in 1929, before this generation was born; we then must rely on the stories we were told by our parents and on government documents, which unfortunately are often in conflict. There are no contemporary, first-hand accounts and no personal recollections of him. With no photographs or other images, we are left only with an imprecise description of Matt, whose grandson Clark Ward Sr. (son of Otis and Carrie Jefferson Ward) is said to have resembled him, according to Clark's daughter Scottie Ward Davis. Clark himself was a handsome, brown-skinned man of medium height, with beautiful, wavy black hair. This is the image of our forefather Matt that we cherish because it gives us something to hold on to.

On the other hand, there are several pictures and many memories of Grandma Ella, as she was affectionately called by her grand- and great-grandchildren, but nearly all of them refer to her in her later years. To date, there are no recollections of a young, vibrant Ella Duncan. Of those who do remember her, some say she was fair skinned; others say she was light-skinned; and still others say she looked white with silky white hair, which she often wore in two thick braids cascading down her back and which the children loved to comb and brush. But these simplistic, semantic differences only point to the probability of Grandma Ella's mulatto heritage—a history we have yet to discover.

Ella Duncan Ward
Matriarch of the Ward family

According to great-grandson Ralph,

> In her later years, Grandma Ella, who
> always wore an apron and a bonnet, was
> a busybody and could not sit still. She
> had a walking stick, which she used to
> threaten to hit anyone and everyone
> who upset her; she would swing it at the
> children who teased and played tricks on
> her to chase them off.

Violet Odessa, sister of Scottie and Dot, remembers how *cute* Grandma Ella was because she was so small, with a friendly personality and a wide, toothless smile. Although she did not talk much, Grandma would often say, "Chillin, y'all do me proud." A devout Christian, she loved her God and her family intensely. In fact, when Grandpa Matt died, she kept her children together, raising them by herself on the farm. And when she grew older, she often spent time between Uniontown with her son Otis and his wife Carrie and Ensley/Birmingham, Alabama, where sons William and Golden had settled and bought homes. The following story is told of how the family finally stopped Grandma Ella from trying to run away from home to get to her two sons. It is told in the dialect of the times.

As she got ol'er an was livin' on da farm, er' da' she wrapped some clothes in a bundle, put dem 'cross her shoulder an set out early er' mo'ning afta brea'fas', tryin' tu walk tu Bunningham tu see her chillin dere. You see, she had don' got ol' and hur min' wuz only set on seein' hur chillin who wuzn' on da farm wid hur. She didn' know no'ing 'bou' how fur it wuz she had tu travel. Well, Ella did dat er' da' til one da' an ol' man come by tu try an' take hur bundle. Dat ol' man wuz really Pearlie dressed up tu skare her so she wudn't try tu leave home agin. After dat, Ella never tried tu run away tu Bunningham agin.

After Otis and Carrie passed, Ella finally got to Birmingham and to Ensley, where her sons took her to live with them until her death on March 21, 1962, at 109 years old.

Despite Matt and Ella's meager beginnings in the Black Belt of Alabama, their descendants have made great economic, political, and educational progress that would have certainly done our ancestors proud. Many of their offspring were, and still are, visionaries and dreamers who earned advanced degrees from prestigious colleges and universities near and far.

We list among them a virtual Who's Who among American institutions of higher learning: the University of Alabama, Alabama A&M University, Alabama State University, Selma University, Southern Polytechnical University, Wallace Community College, University of Birmingham, Stillman College, Auburn University, Booker T. Washington Business School, Walker State Community College, Prairie View A&M University, Blinn Community College, Athens State University, Francis Marion University, University of North Carolina, Duke University, Midlands Technological College, Columbia College, South Carolina State University, Lawson State Community College, Atlanta University, Clark

Atlanta College, Walker State Technology College, Georgia State University, Fisk University, Tennessee State University, Mississippi State University, Mississippi Valley State University, Hinds Community College, Jackson State University, Louisiana State University, Southern University, Grambling University, Xavier University of Louisiana, Dillard University, Northern Arizona University, Arizona State University, University of Oklahoma, Southern Oregon University, University of Phoenix, Walden University, Michigan State University, Wayne State University, Great Lakes Christian College, Rochester College, University of Detroit Mercy, Highland Park Community College, Madonna University, Eastern Michigan University, University of Cincinnati, The Ohio State University, Ohio University, Antioch College, Ashland Theological Seminary, Case Western Reserve University, Central State University, Wilberforce University, Southern Illinois University, Morgan State University, University of Maryland of Baltimore County, Baltimore City Community College, Community College of Baltimore County, Ecumenical Institute of St. Mary's Seminary and University, Bowie State University, Prince Georges Community College, Howard University, Georgetown University, University of Virginia, Hampton University, New York University, The Juilliard School, Cornell University, Hobart and William Smith Colleges, LaSalle University, New Jersey City University, California State University, University of California (Santa Barbara and East Bay), San Francisco State University, St. Mary's College, Western University of Health Services, Modesto Junior College, University of Wisconsin, Washburn University, Brigham Young University, University of London, and Oxford University.

Our educational pursuits have enabled generations of Wards to succeed in the areas of education, Christian ministry, medicine, research administration, corporate administration, library science, entrepreneurship, computer science, information technology, science and technology, athletics (collegiate and professional), politics, banking, financial planning, cosmetology, utilities, industrial engineering, civil engineering, aerospace and avionics engineering, law, real estate law, law enforcement, social work, funeral home services, accounting, literature, publishing, nursing, medical technology, commercial trucking, welding, real estate sales, automotive and mobile home sales, consulting, management, marketing, music, radio and television broadcasting, entertainment, and the list goes on and on.

This family has also served honorably in every branch of the United States armed forces—the air force, army, marines, coast guard, navy, and the national guard.

Yes, we proudly acknowledge that the Wards began in Perry and Dallas Counties, but we have spread our wings beyond to settle in other cities in Alabama, many other states in America, and many countries worldwide. Among those states are Alaska, Arizona, California, Colorado, Florida, Georgia, Hawaii, Illinois, Indiana, Kansas, Maryland, Michigan, Mississippi, Nebraska, Nevada, New York, North Carolina, Ohio, South Carolina, Tennessee, Texas, Washington, and the District of Columbia. Internationally, we've relocated to Canada, England, Germany, China, and the United Arab Emirates.

CHAPTER 6
FROM THIS UNION

Otis Ward (son)

August 1878–September 5, 1955

Isabella or Isabelle Ward (daughter)

July 1884–November 14, 1912

Ludie Ward (son)

June 1885–March 3, 1942

William Ward (son)

December 1890–September 27, 1965

Golden Ward (son)

August 16, 1894–December 23, 1938

Davis Ward (son)[6]

December 25, 1895–April 10, 1976

---

[6] There is disagreement between the authors on including Davis Ward and John Ward as sons of Matt and Ella because several census reports list conflicting information that has not been reconciled.

John Ward (son)[7]
October 1896–1976
Laura Ward (daughter)
August 1898–July 21, 1923

---

[7] Ibid.

CHAPTER 7

OTIS (O. D.) WARD

Eldest child of Matt and Ella

Otis was born in August 1881 and died on September 5, 1955. He married Carrie Ann Jefferson and had

five children: Clark Edward, Lincoln, Violet, Arlene, and Thomas Jefferson. But there were at least three other children conceived outside the marriage: Hattie Mae Turner, John, and A.C.

Born in Perry County, Otis became a Baptist minister, pastoring both the Trinity Baptist Church and Woodlawn Missionary Baptist Church, the family church, for years. The church boasted a membership of about two hundred, mostly young families, the elderly, and some children. Woodlawn held services on the second and fourth Sundays of each month, with Sunday School at 10:00 a.m., and in the tradition of missionary Baptist churches in the South, worship services were always from 11:00 a.m. until 1:00 p.m. According to cousins John and Ralph, services were lively, with a powerful preacher, a pianist, and a choir singing hymns and congregational songs. The services were Spirit-filled with "folk shouting all over the church."

Woodlawn Missionary Baptist Church today
Photos by Ralph Edward Ward, Jr.

Once a year, the Woodlawn Church would have a two-week revival: one week of prayer and one week of preaching. Each day during revival, our family members would stop their work in the fields and attend midweek service at noon. They would later eat lunch, return to the fields, complete their workday, and go back for the evening revival service. Many were saved as they tarried on those hard, wooden benches until they accepted Jesus Christ as their Savior and were baptized in the Holy Spirit. Reflecting on how it used to be, cousin John laments, "Now, we hold revivals only three days a week."

Today, Woodlawn Missionary Baptist Church is a thriving house of worship that holds two family markers on its property: a public school and the family cemetery. For many years, our children attended the Rattan School, which was next to the church and held classes from the first through the sixth grades. And behind Woodlawn Baptist is the Ward Family Cemetery. The first family member to be buried there was Florence Bernice Jordan Ward in 1993. Nearly eighteen years later, her husband, Clark Edward Ward Jr., was laid to rest beside her in 2011. Among the others interred in the family cemetery are Hardie Lee and Minnie Ward, Sylvester Ward, Tommie Ward Sr., and Tommie Ward Jr.

Notably, Matt and Ella are buried in the Woodlawn Cemetery associated with the church.

The late pastor of Woodlawn Baptist, Rev. Otis Ward—Pa or Pop, as he was called by his grandchildren—is described as a handsome charmer who was highly intelligent, wise, and articulate, yet soft-spoken. Grandson Ralph remembers that he could ask him anything and his grandfather would have the answers because he kept a trunk full of books that he used as references. In addition, Pa owned a gas station and a country store and would jokingly bribe the children with goodies from the store. It is said that Otis also made money by buying cheese, crackers, and meat in bulk, which he then sold to other colored families in the area who could only afford it at a reduced price.

An astute businessman and outstanding farmer with no formal education, O.D. was one of the first major Black landowners in Browns. Once when he attempted to buy additional land in another community, he found that the deeds were not cleared on the land on which he had put money down. (Because we know how transactions like this worked during those times, there's no telling what really motivated those who refused to sell to him.) But Pa was able to get his money back and later successfully purchase four hundred acres in Dallas County so that his children and grandchildren could own plats for their families. In addition, Otis was entrusted with many other acres to lease or rent to other colored people, collect the money, and give it to the white landowners. His son, Clark Ward Sr., followed in his footsteps because of his father's sterling reputation. Later, Ma Carrie, or Mommee, bought another thirty acres for the family with a gift she received from an aunt.

In a letter written November 4, 1953, to his younger daughter, Otis laid out how he wanted to keep the land in the family in perpetuity.

Brooks Ala
R-1-Box 106
nov 4th – 1953

Dear Daughter

Some time ago I recd a letter from you being the first one in a long time. Dear you Dont no how glad I was, ever to Read it. from you it put new feeling on me. now listen this is one all verry well except moma & She is holding her own verry well no better I hop this will fin you & your family o.k. Also I call Teo. a week ago & talked to him & was made felt good over his conversasion with me & Since them I got a card from him yesterday & at the Some that I was writing him inregard of my aims to you all. also told him that

Had 160. acrs of Land & that
I could Sell of 80- acrs of
it & that would 80. acrs House
& Wiee pasture all paid for & no
Det on it But to haed to the
160.acr That would mean 40-
Acr piece to each of you. all in
Case of My Death But you all
Wiee ow $775.00 each to Stay with
& intress at 8 ed end but it will
Come down every year from
time you Start your payment
& that wiee Start Dec 5th 1955
He Tald me to haed all of it
Beet listen I am giting alder
Every Day & your moith is too. & I
Wont you all to have this plan
& your childrus after my Deth &
I am going to have my will

it now to you All. Also I have
Seen Lawer Johnso yesterday
he told me that he will do it for
$10.00 $250. each what ever amt
it put into Will. Now rember
80 acr no dets. 160. acr. $ 75.00
each But you got about 15
years to finish paying for it
paying som making it lesser
every year look through it
Last rember the Lower say.
that your mother will have
the Home House en case of my
Death her life Time & that
you all will have to give her
part of what ever you all
make on the Moss Grove
place that will be untill
She is dead & Then you all
But the place cont be

be Said unless to eath
other

This Mass Grove place will
to Clark D. Ward & his airs
to Violet Ward Cook & her airs
to arleoun Ward Smith & her airs
to Thomas J. Ward & his airs
your all cont Sell the
Mass grove place to
no one but yours Self.
Becauss its your childrs
Childres. this place

(Mass Grove place)

Write Soon

yours

Jarthe

O D Ward

85

According to John and Ralph, these acres and hundreds more remain in the Ward family today because siblings have retained ownership while others continue to live on the land purchased by our ancestors, who centuries ago dreamed of keeping the land in the Ward family.

On that land, Otis and Carrie's wood-framed home, with windows on swing-out hinges, was filled with lots of books and lots of love. Arlene's daughter Jaki remembers the summers spent with her grandparents this way:

As a child, I knew my grandparents loved me. And I loved them so much that I never wanted to return home to Cincinnati when summer ended. It was fun playing with my cousins Vater, Dot, and Myrt, pretending to be a country girl picking only a corner of a bag of cotton, touching prickly okra, and digging up sweet potatoes. They made me feel I was doing something special even though I didn't like dirt, flies, bees, or any kind of bug. And I didn't like being hot in that blazing Alabama sun. But my cousins showered me with so much love that I looked past those distractions. My Pop and Mommee, in their sweet, peaceful way, also loved me and made me feel safe.

Yes, Pop and Mommee's home was filled with lots of love and lots of books, but it was also filled with lots of cats that perched on the rafters of the wood-framed house and peered down as the family cooked and ate in the kitchen. Jaki also recalls an incident when she and her cousins were eating breakfast one morning and she dropped food on her bare thigh.

Before I could wipe it off, within seconds, a skinny white cat swooped down, snatched the food off my leg, and sprang back up to the rafter. Everyone laughed; I cried. That was the day I stopped liking cats because *hate* is too strong a word.

Otis's wife **Carrie Jefferson Ward**, called Ma Carrie

or Mommee (born in 1880; died in 1956), attended the public schools of Talladega, Alabama, where she completed the eleventh grade and later became an elementary school teacher. She was said to have a strong, handsome face and often wore her hair in a bun twisted on the back, which accentuated her austere, American Indian-like features. Her skin was smooth, dark brown, and tight from the Alabama sun. A matriarch in the truest sense, she was a take-charge, strong-willed, no-nonsense person who loved her family and helped her husband on the farm, raising their own children and helping raise other generations of Wards.

Loving and perhaps overly protective, Carrie cared about her offspring, advising and helping son Jake with his nine children, visiting every day with her daughter Violet Ward Cooke, and excitedly preparing for son Thomas Jefferson ("T") and daughter Arlene when they returned from Ohio. And when they did, as always, she cooked wonderful meals—she was a great cook—on that old wood-burning stove, especially big, country breakfasts of fresh biscuits from scratch and fresh chicken from the yard (which she would catch herself, wring its neck until it died, defeather, and clean for cooking—all in time for breakfast), and rice smothered in thick, savory gravy. Also, her chicken and dumplings was a favorite dish along with delicious desserts. In fact, Carrie was such a good cook that her reputation preceded her and drew people from near and far who frequently stopped by just to eat.

Otis and Carrie were married for fifty-five years and died within six months of each other. Pop died on September 5, 1955; then, Ma Carrie passed on March 6, 1956.

Family legend has it that the Reverend Otis (O.D.) Ward stopped preaching and pastoring the Trinity Baptist Church and Woodlawn Missionary Baptist Church because his no-nonsense wife Carrie Jefferson Ward would sit on the front bench at church on Sundays and roll her eyes at him in disgust, perhaps because of his personal indiscretions or hypocrisy in not living up to the Word he preached.

OTIS AND CARRIE'S CHILDREN AND THEIR CHILDREN

Violet (Bie) Ward (July 14, 1903–May 20, 1984), the oldest child of Odie and Carrie, married William Ervin Cooke (September 5, 1899—December 1983). From this union, they had eight children: twins Lucie Emma and Otis, Ernestine, Addie Jewel, Mildred, Bessie Mae, Thomas, and Douglas.

Born in Uniontown, Violet or Bie was said to be *biblical* because she always talked about the Lord, referencing everything to being like Jesus and preparing to live forever in eternity with Him. A God-fearing woman, Violet united with her father's church, Woodlawn Missionary Baptist Church, in her hometown in 1918. She served faithfully for fifty-five years as a deaconess, on the mother's board, and as a member of the missionary society, she was also a counselor, teacher, and a Bible student. After the death of her beloved William, she moved to Cincinnati to Live with her daughter Lucie, where she joined Bethlehem Baptist Church on Sunday, May 20, 1984.

And, by the providence of Almighty God, Violet Ward Cooke was called home to be with her Lord on May 20, 1984.

In remembering his Papa, Larry describes his grandfather as a "man of men" who was always there for his family. William Ervin Cooke, known as Toots, was a lover of God and his family and a devout deacon in his church. He was also very athletic and was a catcher in the Negro Baseball League with the Birmingham Clowns (*yes*, that was their name); he had a unique talent for catching a ball with the same hand that he threw with. William remained athletic even at an old age, still able to run long distances with great speed. After working in the steel mills of Bessemer, he bought land and started a farm, where he hired his children and grandchildren to work. And, much to Larry's surprise, his grandfather actually paid them for their labor and often treated them to weekly trips to town—to Uniontown.

Lucie Emma (Honey) Cooke (October 4, 1922–August 21, 2006), the oldest of eight children, was born in Perry County. She became her mother's helper around the house—not the fields! She would do much of the cleaning and cooking, and she could clean and cook like no other. Among her specialties were her buttery pound cakes and cheesy macaroni and cheese. Many also loved her hot, sweet, fluffy homemade rolls. A born homemaker, Lucie lovingly helped raise her twin brother Otis's four children after his death in 1949.

Honey, as she was called, confessed Christ at an early age and had a personal walk with God all her life. When she moved to Cincinnati, she became a faithful member of Bethlehem Baptist Church, where she gave untiring service for more than sixty years and was active in missionary work. Lucie knew the Lord and was a praying mother, often seen on her knees crying out to God, beseeching the Lord for her children. Son Larry recalls that his mother taught them the way of Jesus, how to pray, and how to survive honorably, even during the worst of times. Like the virtuous woman of Proverbs 31:27-30, she is praised:

> *She looketh well to the ways of her household, and eateth not the bread of idleness. Her children arise up and call her blessed; her husband also, and he praiseth her. Many daughters have done virtuously, but thou excellest them all. Favour is deceitful, and beauty is vain, but a woman that feareth the Lord, she shall be praised.*

Lucie married James McCall from Haynesville, Alabama, a descendant of the legendary American Wild West character John Henry "Doc" Holliday, the dentist, gambler, and gunfighter. Holliday, along with Wyatt Earp, took part in the infamous gunfight at the O.K. Corral in October 1881. And, as if true to his heritage, James, who feared no one, was also a fighter, not with guns but with fists. He did, in fact, do a lot of fighting and was finally chased out of Alabama for fighting repeatedly with white people. So he left his hometown and made his way to Cincinnati, where he worked on the railroad and later met and married Lucie Cooke. Together, they had five children, "four stair steps and one thirteen years younger": Larry, James Jr., Gwendolyn, Carolyn, and Barrett. Larry says his father was loving and caring, demonstrating strong family values and teaching them how to stand up for themselves and not be afraid. He taught his boys how to fish, hunt, and play baseball since at one time he was known throughout the South as an outstanding pitcher and outfielder.

Having a mother and father in the home, Larry believes, provided a loving support system for them, one that continues today for the siblings who host family meals and plan McCall family vacations together. All are blessed to have been educated; obtained great jobs; and achieved success in the workplace, church, and community while holding onto the faith of their ancestors.

- Larry (LD) McCall (June 3, 1946) married Mary Johnson and was a career firefighter. He served for thirty years and retired in 2002. He has two sons. Andre Lamont and his wife Tambi Flye McCall have two sons (Andre Jr. and Trinton) and live in Indianapolis. Larry's other son, Richard Dwight, lives in Cincinnati.

- James (Brother) McCall Jr. (November 30, 1947) married Otero Glass and is the father of NaKeisha and grandfather of two: Jayla Warren and Mark Burns. Brother was a career firefighter and retired from the Cincinnati Fire Department on October 3, 1999. He was blessed to graduate from the University of Cincinnati on the same day in August 1974 as his sister Gwen—he with a Bachelor of Science degree in criminal justice and she with a Bachelor of Arts in education.

- Gwendolyn (Gwenny, Gwen) McCall (December 22, 1948) married Ronnie Cole. They are the parents of Latisha and the grandparents of five. Gwen taught in the public schools of Cincinnati before retiring in 2004.

- Carolyn (Carol) McCall (December 18, 1950) married Hughes Miller, and they are the parents of DeJuane Miller and the grandparents of four. She settled in Dayton, Ohio, and was employed by the US Postal Service for more than twenty-five years.

- Barrett (Bud) McCall (August 3, 1959) married Melody Norris on February 20, 1992, and they are the parents of Barrett Ashton. Bud attended the University of Cincinnati, earning a bachelor's degree in business administration and a Master of Arts in business administration (MBA) in 1981 and 1982, respectively. He retired as a senior manager from the Coca-Cola Company of Atlanta, Georgia, where he worked for over thirty-two years.

Otis Davis (Brother) Cooke (October 4, 1922–February 14, 1949) died at the age of twenty-seven. Named after his maternal grandfather, Otis married Mammie Brooks (1924–June 24, 1951). They had four children who were raised by their grandparents, Violet and William, after the deaths of Otis and Mammie.

- William (Wendell) Cooke and wife Terrie Mae Moore Cooke had three children: Patrice Cooke, Christopher Cooke, and Denise Cooke.

- Otis Marie (Sister) Cooke is married to Paul Lewis; they are the parents of son Paul N. Lewis.

- Carl Davis (Carla) Cooke is the mother of three: Christine White Bruno, Lydia White, and son Pastor Phillip White.

  What is historically significant to the Ward family is that **Pastor Phillip White**, a graduate of the University of Alabama, became the third Black mayor of Uniontown, a town central to our history and just eight miles from where Matt and Ella settled. Rev. White was elected to two terms as mayor, from 2000 to 2008, after having served on the Uniontown City Council for four years.

  He says he was influenced to run because he wanted to see things get done in this small, Black town that was losing population to area industrial communities. To him, the exodus to follow economic opportunities was changing the Black Belt of Alabama and Uniontown, in particular, *causing it to go down*. Because small-town politics had also gotten in the way of progress, Mayor White says he sought to improve the city's quality of life, which had no tax base and low property taxes, by increasing street signage, making infrastructure improvements, and upgrading the water treatment facility. And before his tenure ended, the former mayor had successfully written a grant for two million dollars and signed a consent order with the Alabama Capital

Improvement Fund to repair and upgrade the town's sewer system.

In addition, our cousin and his wife Carla White, a registered nurse, are the owners of Phillip White's Julia L. White Funeral Home in Uniontown, which was established in 1874. He is the lead mortician and funeral director. The funeral home is a family-owned, full-service facility that provides a comfortable yet professional environment for families. With more than thirty years in the funeral business, he and his wife offer grief counseling, preplanning services, creation of obituaries, an in-house flower boutique, cremation services, caskets, cemetery plots, and a headstone monument selection tool.

And as if all of this was not enough, the Reverend Phillip White has *done our ancestors proud* by following in the footsteps of his great-great-grandfather Rev. Otis (O.D.) Ward. Rev. White is the pastor of the Mt. Olive Missionary Baptist Church—The Olive—in Gallion, Alabama, where Jesus is Lord and where God's love is transferred through a ministry of teaching, preaching, praying, healing, and joyfully giving while spiritual gifts are being utilized. Additionally, members are taught to value the Word, to worship the Lord in spirit and in truth, and to love one another as minds are renewed, lives transformed, and life's purposes are found. The Olive is about family growth and God's vision to a blessed church.

- Addie Jewel (Tina or Teeny) Cooke is married to the Rev. James Carter Sr. They have four children: twins Nea and Nina Carter, James Carter II, and Pamela Carter.

Ernestine (Teen) Cooke (October 6, 1923—1996), of Petersburg, Virginia, married Abraham Shepherd.

Thomas Ervin (Boy Baby) Cooke, born in 1926, resides in Atlanta, Georgia.

Addie Jewel (Booty) Cooke Taylor (July 5, 1927—March 11, 2002) was the devoted mother of seven—four girls and three boys. Addie was a devout Christian and long-standing member of New Sardis Primitive Baptist Church of Cleveland, Ohio, where our cousin Rev. A. J. W. Warren once pastored and family members still attend. She was an accomplished singer, often singing in her church and throughout the city. She inspired her children to sing and encouraged each one to play musical instruments. At one time, this musical family became known as The Taylors, singing the praises of our Lord and Savior throughout the area. Later, many of the siblings became international psalmists, entertainers, and performers.

- B. Jean Taylor Rich has three children, Yvette Sharee Taylor, Andre Lamont Taylor, and Davida Janene Taylor; eleven grandchildren; and seven great-grandchildren. Jean is an anointed singer.

- Brenda Joyce Taylor Gard, a powerful singer, is the mother of Jerrita Taylor and Princess Gard Cunningham, grandmother of three, and great-grandmother of one.

- Bernard Ervin (Beloyd) Taylor (September 7, 1952–January 13, 2014) was a quintessential guitarist, songwriter, and vocalist. Few would know he also played the flute and harmonica. However, many are aware that our cousin was a significant part of the sound and music of the 1980s musical powerhouse Earth, Wind & Fire. Although Bernard began his career playing guitar with the group S.O.U.L (Sounds of Unity and Love) in his hometown, he joined EWF after co-writing the mega-hit "Getaway," which sold over a million copies worldwide. He also contributed to many of the group's top albums, such as *Spirit* (1976) and *Raise!* (1981), writing the tracks for "Lady Sun," "You Are a Winner," "Changing Times," "Spread Your Love," and "Heart to Heart."

    Not only did Beloyd, a stage name given him by a group member, perform with Earth, Wind & Fire, but he composed and recorded his own music—singing all the vocals—in his soulful, melodious tones. The best example is "Get into Your Life" recorded on the 20th Century Records label. For many, it is his signature song, both literally and figuratively.

His musical credits, as either vocalist or percussionist, are lengthy and include working in 1976 with Donald Byrd, renowned jazz trumpeter and vocalist, and in 1978 with Grammy-award winning jazz-fusion saxophonist Gary Bartz. Bernard also played and traveled with the smooth jazz group Hiroshima and performed with R&B legend Chaka Khan.

Bernard was the father of Bernard Forte Taylor, Jewel Taylor Mancha, Taniece Hilliard, and Tamica Hilliard, and he had six grandchildren, many of whom carry on their father and grandfather's legacy.

• Pastor Cheryl Diane Taylor Frazier and husband Apostle Glenn Curtis Frazier Sr., are a ministry team, having founded Beracah Faith Ministries International in May 2001 in Temecula, California. It is a multicultural, non-denominational church with a family outreach mission. They devote themselves to advancing the Word of God and to the mission of "developing people of influence and integrity for the kingdom of Christ." Beracah Faith Ministries is a Spirit-filled, Spirit-led "place where blessings flow" because worshippers encounter the presence of Almighty God in that holy place.

Pastor Cheryl, our cousin, is a powerful prophetic preacher and psalmist. Appointed for such a time as this, Cheryl shares her gifts with the world through the preached Word and through song, having ministered with many of today's leading faith leaders. They include Bishop T.D. Jakes of the Potter's House of Dallas, Texas; Dr. Creflo Dollar of the World Changers Church International of College Park, Georgia; and Pastor Rod Parsley of World Harvest Church in Canal Winchester, Ohio, near Columbus. One only needs to hear Pastor Cheryl sing "In the Name of the Lord," "I Love You, Lord," or "He Knows How Much We Can Bear" to know that this is a vessel anointed by God.

Her husband, Apostle Frazier, shares in a post on Apostles and Prophets Network about the power of his anointed life partner:

> I truly praise God that He has blessed me to be married to such a powerfully anointed woman and voice as Cheryl Frazier. Her voice has been used to bring people back out of comas and the Lord even used her to literally "raise me from the dead" on January 31, 2002, when I literally fell dead in our hotel room while in Atlanta. To say the least, I'm

eternally grateful for such a woman. She has
been and is still a tremendous blessing to the
Body of Christ around the world.

Apostle Glenn and Pastor Cheryl Frazier have two
sons, Glenn Jr. and Kevin; six grandchildren; and one
great granddaughter.

- Evangelist Wendy Ladell Taylor Hairston is in ministry
  with her husband, Evangelist Wendell Hairston.
  Evangelist Wendy serves as the music director at
  Beracah Faith Ministries International, the church
  pastored by her sister and brother-in-law. Our cousin
  Wendy is accomplished on the keyboard and string
  instruments. Professionally, she is a registered nurse
  and a special education teacher. She is the mother of
  Deonna Hairston and Deon Hairston.

- Willie Earl Taylor (March 6, 1956–March 14, 2018)
  played congas.

- Jeffrey Taylor

The Taylors are third-generation musicians, following in the
path of their matriarch, Addie Jewel Cooke Taylor: Glenn
"Mann" Frazier Jr. is a drummer for the group Liquid Blue
Band; Kevin Frazier plays keyboard; Deon Hairston is a
drummer and is active in theater in California; Andre Ski

Taylor, a keyboardist and drummer, also has his own T-shirt business called Congratulations; and Jewell Taylor Mancha plays keyboard. According to Jean Taylor Rich, "All our sons and daughters sing."

Mildred (Ree) Cooke (October 5, 1932) of Wilberforce, Ohio, is a college graduate and was married to the late Cleophus Paul Miree. They had two children, Paul Harvey and Karen.

Bessie Mae Cooke (1933–January 10, 1985) married Don Devan Phillips and was the mother of Belinda Gail Phillips. Bessie accepted Christ at an early age and joined Woodlawn Baptist Church, her family church, where she was a faithful member until she married and moved to Atlanta, Georgia. She then united with the Friendship Baptist Church in College Park, Georgia.

She attended Selma University and Alabama A&M University in Huntsville, where she received her Bachelor of Science degree in social studies. She conducted additional studies at Georgia State University in Atlanta. She began her teaching career in Akron, Alabama, and was later employed by the Fulton County Board of Education. As a teacher, she was best described as a role model and a youth motivator with an exuberant personality.

Douglas Lee (Doug) Cooke of Montgomery, Alabama (December 28, 1934—2012) graduated from high school and enlisted in the military.

Clark Edward (Jake) Ward Sr. (December 28, 1906–January 13, 1960) remained on the family compound and farmed all his life. Born in Dallas County, Clark married his first wife, Jerline Sanders (born in 1906), and they had four children: Clark Edward Jr. (Ed), Violet Odessa (Sister), Hardie Lee (Lee), and Scottie Mae (Scott).

After the death of Jerline at an early age, Jake married Pearlie Mae Black (April 4, 1914–July 18, 2007) from Uniontown. Together, they had five children: John Lee, Dorothy Ree (Dot), Myrtis Joann (Myrt), Willie Jean (Jean), and Walter Nevater (Vater). All their offspring were raised together on the farm in Browns/Uniontown, Dallas County, Alabama.

Strict disciplinarians, Clark and Pearlie Mae were watchful, loving parents who devoted their lives to raising their nine children and working from sunup to sundown picking cotton, corn, okra, sweet potatoes, and other crops. They instilled high morals, honesty, and work ethics, teaching the children to strive to be their best. Daughter Violet Odessa recalls, "Daddy wanted us to represent the Ward family name, so all his time was spent telling us how to act." Their Christian values were a priority as together they attended the family church every Sunday, with Jake serving as chairman of the deacon board, helping to run the church, and teaching Sunday School and Pearlie Mae working with the missionary society. All their children accepted Jesus Christ as their Lord and Savior and participated in special activities and programs because church was their spiritual and social outlet.

All nine children looked up to their father and thought he "was the most important, most intelligent man on earth." Although he only completed school through the eighth grade, Jake became an outstanding business-farmer who studied the growth of his crops and animals to the extent of being among the most highly successful Black farmers in the county. Jake and his family were industrious, growing most of the fruits, vegetables, and meats that were sold. They also made their own syrup and butter from clabber milk. In addition, they sold milk to the Uniontown Creamery from the cows they raised. And because he was such a success, Jake was able to hire other people in the community to help work his fields. He was highly respected in the church and community and among the segregated business community.

During the early years of segregation, Clark Ward Sr. understood the position of Negroes in the Deep South. To this end, he developed a successful approach to dealing with the white people to whom he sold his produce despite facing blatant racism in the Black Belt. Even though he was a proud, strong man, he did not challenge white people, yet he was straightforward and dealt with them with integrity. (Of course, no one knows the humiliation that he experienced as a Negro in the white man's world, but, according to daughter Dot, he held his head high, stood his ground, and set high standards for his family.) The name Clark Ward was always spoken with respect and dignity. He gained white people's confidence by being trustworthy and dependable. His farm was often identified as one of the top farms in the county. For many years, he received recognition for ginning the first bale of cotton in the community, literally making him the *Cotton King of Dallas County.*

Jake's second wife Pearlie, affectionately known as Ma Pearl, worked diligently beside her husband on the farm until his death in 1960. She was described by the family as humorous and full of wisdom. After Jake passed, she stayed on the farm another three years, then moved to Oakland, California, to be with her daughters, Dot and Myrtis (Myrt) Ward Davis. In California, Pearlie lived a very productive life working in the community and in the church—The Church by the Side of the Road in Berkeley. She served on the usher board and pastor's aide committee and was president of the Feed the Needy ministry. Everyone loved her and enjoyed being in her company. She loved her family and helping others, especially children. Some of her *pearls of wisdom* include, "If you have a problem with someone, turn it over to the Lord and He will fix it. You just do right yourself." Also, she would often say, "As long as you can get up in the morning, bathe your own body, and dress yourself, then you are truly blessed."

Clark's boys stayed on the farm, becoming successful farmers just like their father, but after high school and college, all the girls moved away, either following their husbands or simply looking for better job opportunities. Violet Odessa (Sister) moved to Cincinnati; Scottie to Cleveland; Dot and Myrt to California; Jean to Tuskegee until her death at the age of twenty-six; and Vater went to business college in Birmingham and stayed there after she married.

Clark Edward (Ed) Ward Jr. (January 31, 1927–October 25, 2011) was the oldest of Clark Sr. and Jerline Sanders's children. Ed confessed Christ at an early age and joined the family church in Uniontown, serving as both a trustee and a choir member for many years.

At nineteen years old, he married Florence Bernice Jordan of Marion Junction. Ed and Bernice had seven children, often called *farmhands*: Sylvester, Ralph Edward Sr., George Donald, Tommie Lincoln, Eddie Matthew, Jonathan, and Barbara Jean. These farmhands were very motivated to get off the farm, which they eventually did, to pursue their dreams. Ed also fathered another son, Joe Nathan Whitt.

Ed was of average height with a medium build and a pleasant personality. According to his only daughter, Barbara, her father always had a smile on his face. She says he was also full of wisdom and would instruct his children on how to live productive, successful lives. Among his many wise sayings are these:

- "Never take a noose off another man's neck and put it around yours."
- "Don't bow to no man."
- "Stay away from small-minded people because they'll have you thinking just like them."
- "Always manage your money because the man with the money is the man with the power."
- "It's better to be in the position to buy something than to buy it, because you can always buy something if you're in position."
- "Everybody wants your money, so you best try to keep as much of it as you can."

This man of wisdom was a consummate entrepreneur with a passion for farming. Reportedly, he worked all the time and farmed every year from 1946 through the fall of 2010, when he began to experience health issues. "He worked all the time and he worked us, too," says older son Ralph, who admits that because he himself had to work throughout his childhood, he learned how to become financially secure and care for himself and his family. He saw his father commit everything to his family and his farm. As a farmer, Clark Jr. raised crops and livestock, including but not limited to okra, soybeans, and cows, and he sold hay, wood and coal. He operated his business with integrity; when he'd sell items that were measured by weight, he'd have his children throw in extra to make sure his customers were getting at least what they paid for.

He was indeed a dedicated farmer and salesman, while Bernice, said to be a dependable, hard worker, was overseer and *enforcer*, managing the children and the farm workers. And even though Bernice ran the business, she always respected her husband and deferred to him as the man of the house. When she instructed the children, she always said, "Ed said," but, when Ed got home, he would be surprised that chores were done. She taught her sons and daughter to lead by example and would tell them, "Y'all better get out there [to the fields] first because I can't get the workers to go if y'all ain't working."

The dedication of this husband-wife team led to Ed's becoming one of the first in many things: the *first* Black man in the area to sell okra to grocery store warehouses in Birmingham, namely to Bruno's Warehouse, Food World, as well as to the farmers market and other privately owned producers. He was also the *first* Black man in the county to own a Black Angus bull and the *first* Black man to build a brick house that was fully paid for upon completion of construction.

Clark Edward Ward Jr. was blessed with eighty-four wonderful years of sound health and mind and eight successful children:

- Sylvester (Ves) Ward (December 3, 1946–May 9, 1973) married Jeannie E. Walker. Sylvester served his country in the US Air Force, where he obtained the rank of staff sergeant and became a certified body, fender, and paint specialist. After leaving the air force, he worked at Ted Jenson Body and Paint Shop in Selma, Alabama, where he was recognized for building a vehicle from two wrecked (totaled) automobiles. Cutting the frames in half, he took the two good halves and welded them together to make one good, usable automobile. Afterward, he became a successful entrepreneur, building and operating the Ward Paint and Body Shop. Part of his business included buying and repairing wrecked cars for resale.

  Tragically, one evening while working on a vehicle, Ves was severely burned in an explosion that occurred while he was welding a car he was repairing. While tack welding on this car, sparks from the torch entered a nearby five gallon can of paint thinner, which ultimately exploded, severely injuring Sylvester and his fourteen-year-old brother Eddie. Their brother George sustained minor injuries to his arm, and their uncle John sustained serious injuries to his hands. Ves later passed away from his injuries at the age of twenty-six. His business was then passed on to his brother Tommy.

- Ralph Edward Ward Sr. (born March 12, 1948) graduated from Robert C. Hatch High School and then enlisted in the US Army, where he was deployed and served his country during the Vietnam War. After completing his military tour of duty, he enrolled at Lawson State Community College, where he became a certified electrician. Ralph was employed at Pullman Standard, Sloss Furnace, and other places before becoming a senior automotive salesman with Edwards Chevrolet in Birmingham until his retirement.

  Ralph is married to Shirley Annette Whitely, a retired registered nurse; they have two sons.

  Ralph Edward Ward Jr. was born in Birmingham on September 11, 1979. He graduated from Huffman High School in Huffman, Alabama. Upon graduation, he enrolled in Dillard University in New Orleans, Louisiana, but later transferred to Tennessee State University in Nashville, earning a Bachelor of Science degree in political science. Like his father and grandfather, he is naturally gifted in the area of sales. He has been successfully employed in sales and in management with various wireless service providers for over fifteen years, the last six years with T-Mobile Wireless. Ralph dearly loves the Ward family and travels coast to coast to support them during both good and difficult times.

Justin DeVaughn Ward was born on February 24, 1983, in Birmingham. After graduating from Huffman High School, he enrolled at Auburn University in Auburn, Alabama, where he earned a Bachelor of Arts degree in English. It was there that he met his future wife, Jacquetta Allen. Justin later earned a master's degree in instructional design and technology from Walden University. He is an educator, author, motivational speaker, and entrepreneur. He is also an active worship leader in the children's ministry in his church.

Justin and Jacquetta Allen Ward are the parents of two daughters, Jamari DeVaughn Ward (May 20, 2007), a percussionist in the band at her school and an avid reader, and Juliette Alyce Ward (March 27, 2010), who also loves to read and sings in her school's choir. Both girls have accepted Jesus Christ as their Lord and Savior and are active in church activities.

- Joe Nathan Whitt, a native of Browns, Alabama, where Madison and Ella Ward settled, was born on March 19, 1950. He and his family relocated to Mobile, Alabama, where he was raised by his mother, stepfather, and his grandparents. After graduating from Blount High School in 1968, he enrolled at Alabama State University, enjoying an outstanding football career until 1972, when he graduated with a Bachelor of Science degree with a double major in business administration and history. He continued his education at Alabama State and earned his master's degree in business administration (MBA) in 1976. After college, Joe accepted a position as a driver with UPS, and while he appreciated the benefits of the job, it was not his dream job. He later joined the staff of Robert E. Lee High School in Montgomery as an assistant football and head wrestling coach.

From 1981 until 2005, he was an assistant football coach at Auburn University, then becoming an assistant athletic director for the football program. He retired from AU in 2015. That same year, his alma mater, Alabama State University, appointed him to serve on the school's board of trustees.

Joe has enjoyed an illustrious coaching career in athletics and has been inducted into several area sports halls of fame, including Blount High School and Robert E. Lee High School, and the city of Mobile Sports Hall of Fame. Then, in January 2019, Joe Nathan Whitt received the American Football Coaches Lifetime Achievement Award for outstanding service.

He and his wife, Ethel, a retired Lee County corrections administrator in Opelika, Alabama, live in Auburn. They are the parents of a daughter, NaKesha Dionne Whitt, and a son, Joseph Barrington Whitt.

NaKesha Dionne Whitt (August 1, 1977) has a diploma from Auburn High School and a Bachelor of Science degree in early childhood education from Auburn University. She has been an elementary school teacher for nearly twenty years. Dionne, who loves children, is the mother of a beautiful set of twins: Nathan Devin and Michael Michelle.

Joseph Barrington Whitt is called Joe-Joe by his family and friends. Keeping with his family's tradition of attending Auburn University, where his father was a football coach and his sister Dionne received her degree, Joe-Joe graduated from AU with a Bachelor of Science degree in communications, with a minor in business.

Likewise, he followed his father's path into athletics and began coaching at the Citadel, a military college in South Carolina. Later, he joined the staff at the University of Louisville. Advancing in his career to the pinnacle of professional athletics, he is now a successful coach in the National Football League (NFL). His career is one of high achievement after having been a coach for the Atlanta Falcons and the Green Bay Packers. Currently, he is on the coaching staff of the Cleveland Browns.

Joe-Joe has been married to Ericka for fifteen years, and they have three children: Joseph Jr., age thirteen; Ava, ten; and Zoë, six.

- George Donald Ward, born on December 14, 1951, graduated from Robert C. Hatch High School in 1970. He confessed Christ at an early age and joined the family church in Uniontown. Some years later, after the death of his brother Sylvester, he too enlisted in the US Air Force and was honorably discharged after his tour of duty. He later enrolled at Wallace Community College in Selma, Alabama, receiving his certification in welding. As a certified welder, he obtained employment with the Pullman Standard Company until it shut down. George then returned to his hometown, where he has resided since.

  In the 1970s, he designed and built a mobile engine pulley that was used to pull engines out of vehicles. At that time, there were none like his design, but they are more common today. Unfortunately, George did not register his design for a patent. Multi-talented, he is a self-taught, accomplished bass and lead guitarist who loves to sing, something he does very well. He is also an excellent artist who can draw anything. When he was younger, he was a skilled gymnast who could do all sorts of flips as well as walk on his hands.

  George is the father of four: Virginia, Georgette,

and twins Adrienne Denise and Adrienne Sharrell Ward.

- Tommy Lincoln Ward (October 6, 1955–July 6, 2006) attended the same high school as his brothers and later enrolled in the US Job Corps. He was mechanically inclined at a very early age. His sister Barbara says that, once, Tommy took the engine from their parents' lawnmower and put it on his bicycle. Then one day he came riding from behind the house on his bike, which was being powered by the small engine he had taken from the lawnmower. The family was stunned as they watched him speed around. This was the beginning of his love for street racing, often having the "car to beat"! People would say, "Don't mess with T Ward" because he usually had the fastest car or motorcycle in the area.

  Tommy became well known as a great mechanic, repairing and rebuilding engines and doing other car repairs. After the passing of his oldest brother Sylvester, he took an interest in auto body repair, pushing aside his mechanical abilities. He was self-trained and became one of the best body repairmen and painters in the area. He was like his dad in that he never wanted to work for anyone else. Tommy gave up his body repair business due to health issues and passed away on July 6, 2006.

Tommie Ward was born in October 1973 and was raised by his grandparents Ed and Bernice as their own. He attended the Uniontown Elementary School until his life ended early due to complications from a brain tumor in December 1983.

Michael Ward, like his father, is a very skilled paint and body and paint specialist.

Maurice Cash attended Robert C. Hatch High School in Uniontown.

Teresa Jackson was born in Alabama in 1976 but attended Glenville High School in Cleveland, Ohio. She later enrolled in cosmetology school and is very passionate about hair, makeup, and fashion. Currently, she works for an electric company in Cleveland. Her son, Terrance Hurt, a graduate of Richmond Heights High School, enrolled in trade school and earned his certification in welding. He is a single father raising Skylar, a precocious and charismatic daughter. His son Dymetrest Barnfield was born and raised in Fort Wayne, Indiana.

- Eddie Matthew Ward was born on November 16, 1959, in Browns. He accepted Christ as his Savior at an early age and was very active in the Ward family church. In

1981, he followed in his brothers' tradition by graduating from Robert C. Hatch High School; five years later, after working on the farm with his father, Eddie decided to pursue his dream of becoming a truck driver. He enrolled in Walker State Community College, earning a commercial driver's license (CDL). Immediately upon completion, Eddie obtained employment with Material Delivery Service. In 1998, he was recognized by ECS Underwriting, a provider of environmental insurance, as the best truck driver for safety, service, and performance from among 178 drivers nationwide. He continues to be among the best drivers today and is accident-free after thirty-two years of driving. Eddie continues to reside in Uniontown, where he owns and operates a paint and body shop.

- Jonathan (Joe) Ward was born in Browns, Alabama, on January 11, 1963. Like most of his family, he joined the Woodlawn Missionary Baptist Church and in 1981 graduated from the Robert C. Hatch High School. Joe earned an academic scholarship from Jackson State University in Jackson, Mississippi, earning a Bachelor of Science degree in business finance. He later accepted a position as assistant financial aid director at Meharry Medical College in Nashville, Tennessee. Joe continued his education at Atlanta University (currently Clark Atlanta University), receiving a Master of Business

Administration, or MBA, with a concentration in finance. Upon graduating from AU, Joe went to work as a financial analyst and senior project director for Union Pacific Railroad in Omaha, Nebraska. Later accepting a position as a senior business analyst for Shell Oil Products, he moved to Houston, Texas, where he met and married Dr. Davida Manor, an emergency room physician in Houston. They have two daughters, Golden and Jonelle. The family moved to El Paso, where they partnered in opening two emergency centers, which they later sold. Joe also serves as general manager and president of the Harris County Metropolitan Utility District.

Jalyn Ward is the older of the twins, born on January 26, 1998 in Omaha. She graduated from Westfield High School in Houston in 2015 and later enrolled at Blinn Community College in Brenham, Texas, to study criminal justice. Jalyn is currently continuing the family tradition of entrepreneurship, operating a full-service beauty salon.

Kalyn Ward, like her sister, graduated from Westfield High. She also attended Blinn Community College and transferred to Prairie View A&M University to obtain a bachelor's degree in health science (to be awarded in August 2019).

Kalyn plans to work in hospital administration and obtain her master's in health science. Like her twin, Kalyn is in the beauty field with a successful eyelash business.

Golden Ward and her sister Jonelle Ward were born in Houston and have very busy schedules; they're enrolled in ballet, piano, art and gymnastics. Jonelle is also in the gifted education program and in the dual language (English/Spanish) program at their school. In addition to grade school, they're active in church, singing in the children's choir.

• Barbara Jean Ward was born in Tuskegee, Alabama, on March 14, 1965. She came to Christ as a child in the Woodlawn Baptist Church. In 1983, she graduated from Robert C. Hatch and enrolled at Jackson State University in Jackson, Mississippi. As many young people do, she followed her heart after one semester and transferred to Alabama A&M University (AAMU) in Normal, Alabama.

In October 1985, she married and gave birth to a son, Wayne A. Early Jr., on April 27, 1986. She and her son went on military tour of duty with her then husband until he was medically evacuated back to the United States. After sitting out of school for two years to care for her son, Barbara went back to AAMU, where she graduated cum laude with a bachelor's degree in mathematics in May 1989. That same year, she accepted a position as a statistician with the United States Department of Agriculture (USDA), National Agriculture Statistics Service (NASS) in Annapolis, Maryland. She then transferred to the Jackson, Mississippi, field office to be closer to her family as her mother, Bernice, had various health issues. She was divorced in June 1992 and lost her mother months later in March 1993. Barbara made the decision to remain in Mississippi, where she gave birth to her second son, Jordan Odom, in February 1996. She lived there for twenty-two years until her father passed in October 2011. Less than a year later, she accepted a position with her current agency, which relocated her to headquarters in the Washington, DC area, where she lives in Bowie, Maryland.

Wayne Early Jr., was born on April 27, 1986, in Selma, Alabama. After graduating from Callaway High School, class of 2004, in Jackson, Mississippi, Wayne enrolled at Alabama A&M University, where he obtained a Bachelor of Science degree in electrical engineering. After his freshman year at AAUM, he secured a position as a co-op student with the National Security Agency (NSA) in Fort Meade, Maryland. When he returned to the university, he took a position at Systems Management and Production (SMAP) center at the University of Alabama, Huntsville, which allowed him to rotate through several positions on Redstone Arsenal. These positions included working as a systems analyst co-op student at Joint Air-to-Ground Missiles and as an information technology administrator with Red Test Center (RTC). Once Wayne graduated, he accepted a full-time position with RTC; however, he had always dreamed of working and living abroad. In 2013, he secured a position in Kuwait City, Kuwait, as a Department of Army civilian contractor working as service desk administrator. He currently lives and works in Dubai, United Arab Emirates, as a senior systems administrator and engineer.

Wayne's passion for travel has led him to visit more than twenty countries, including Ethiopia, Thailand, Sri Lanka, and Turkey. He also became a landowner and first-time homeowner, closing on both properties on the same day in 2017.

Jordon Odom was born in Flowood, Mississippi. He attended Ridgeland High School in Ridgeland until he and his mom relocated to Maryland. Jordan graduated from Bowie High School in Bowie, Maryland, but his heart was still in Mississippi.

After graduation, Jordan raced back to the South, where he enrolled at Hinds Community College in Raymond, Mississippi. After a year at the community college and some eye-opening life experiences, he transferred to Prince Georges Community College in Largo, Maryland. One semester short of obtaining his associate's degree, he decided that he didn't like school anymore and started working at UPS as a loader and then a driver. He later began working as a FedEx driver, where he has been for two years.

Jordan, like his brother, is both technologically savvy and mechanically inclined and very good at diagnosing automobile issues.

Violet Odessa Ward is the great-granddaughter of Matt and Ella and the second of the four children of Clark Ward Sr. and Jerline Sanders.

Fondly called Sister, Violet was born in Browns, or Uniontown, in 1929. When she was six years old, her mother died, and she and her siblings were cared for by her grandparents Otis and Carrie until her father married Ma Pearl. From this union, five children were born, increasing the blended family to eleven in number. During her early education, Sister attended the Rattan School, a one-room school for grades one through six. At that time, teachers from Rattan lived with the students' families; Sister remembers her teacher, Miss Gram, living with the Wards during the school year.

Because education was also important to Violet's maternal grandparents, Allen and Martha Alice Sanders opened their home in Marion, Alabama, to their grandchildren so that they could have the opportunity to attend Lincoln High School, a private secondary institute founded after the Civil War to educate newly freed slaves to become teachers. Initially established as a tuition-paid school, Lincoln later charged only $4.50 per year. It became known for graduating a remarkable number of students who went on to earn advanced degrees. Violet's graduating class was about fifty students. But in May 1970, the Lincoln School closed—after 103 years—because it merged with a white school, and those parents did not want their children going to a historically *colored* school.

Following her Aunt Arlene, Violet was the second Ward to enroll at Lincoln; her younger sister Scottie Mae also attended. Violet says it was a good experience because it offered so many different activities and classes, like sewing, secretarial classes, workshop for boys, and the famed Little Chorus, which performed before audiences in many northern states. Every morning the students met in the auditorium for prayer. For her, it had the feel of a college campus, with seven buildings, including dormitories, arranged in a beautifully landscaped setting. It provided her the opportunity to meet so many interesting people; for example, for four years, Coretta Scott

King, the late wife of civil rights icon Dr. Martin Luther King Jr., attended Lincoln along with her brother Obadiah Leonard, a classmate of Violet's. As the story goes, each year when school was out for the summer, the Ward children would return to Uniontown to work the farm until the next school session.

Sister's memories of Browns, Alabama, are vivid. She tells of how the Wards had four houses situated near one another where the children could go in and out of each house repeatedly as one big family. She says they owned five horses (one of which was snow white) that they rode within a fenced area of the farm. And on the land was a pond where they caught crawdads and cooked them like shrimp.

Each day from sunup to sundown, as they worked the farm, someone would ring the bell so that those working in the fields would know it was high noon and time for lunch. They could also tell the hour when they could no longer see their shadows, but as the day wore on, their shadows would go out from them and their silhouettes could be seen extending on the ground.

Sister admits that she and farm-work did not go together, but she did reluctantly milk cows, feed pigs and chickens, and work in the fields, picking cotton, okra, and sweet potatoes. She didn't like churning milk to make butter, pumping water from a well, using outhouses, and being without electricity and phones, not even when she went away to high school. To light the house, they used kerosene lamps that emitted an oily smell and cast shadowy glows throughout. In her words, she hated being a *country girl* but wanted to be a *city girl*. So after high school, in search of a better life, Violet moved to Cincinnati, where Aunt Arlene and Uncle T had relocated. There she met and married a handsome, charismatic chef named Harold E. Ridgeway and settled there to raise their four children: Rex, Paula, Darryl, and Melonee. Violet and Harold loved their children and devoted their lives to their well-being.

- Rex Ridgeway is the father of Kimberly Ridgeway, a writer and actress who lives in San Francisco, California.

- Paula Ridgeway married Steve Moore and has three children: Tia, who married Jermaine Rochelle, and they are the parents of Myles, Zacari, Houston, and Brielle); Cedric, a graduate of Tennessee State University; and Anise, the mother of four: Maniyeah, Maliyah, Kevin, and Zariyah. Paula received her bachelor's degree from Ohio University.

- Darryl Ridgeway is in construction. He is the father of four children: Stacey Forde (married to Wade Forde Sr.; they are the parents of Olivia, Wade Jr., and Laila); Melody (mother of Morgan); Deonte (father of Deonte Jr. and Elianna); and Darryl Jr. (DJ).

- Melonee (NeeNee) Ridgeway graduated from Central State University in Wilberforce, Ohio, with a Bachelor of Science in social work. With great humility, she describes herself as a *wonderful and loving auntie.*

Hardie Lee Ward (January 10, 1930–April 15, 2002) was the younger son of Clark and Jerline. He married Minnie Waddy on May 17, 1952, and to this union three children were born— Shirley Ann, Tharone Brenford, and Vinetta Yvette.

Lee, as he was known, accepted Christ in 1940 and joined Woodlawn Baptist. Lee loved the Lord and sang His praises with his beautiful, melodious voice. He, along with his brother Clark Jr. and Clifton Swain, Manson Starks, and Joe Dansby formed a glee club known as the Spiritual Five. They sang at churches in the community and periodically at Demopolis Radio Station during the spiritual hour of funeral home broadcasts.

Like his father Jake, Lee was a successful farmer and businessman. He was known as the Okra King in his community and was blessed to sell his produce in Birmingham, Montgomery, and Tuscaloosa, Alabama. He provided jobs for more than two hundred workers (graders, pickers, field walkers, record keepers, and truck drivers) during the farming season. Later during his career, he grew soybeans and sold the crop to local white vendors.

From 1987 to 2002, he owned a used car dealership. This was a business he loved, and he had a natural talent for selling cars. For fifteen years, he sold cars in his neighborhood and surrounding areas, providing reasonably priced automobiles and services to friends and neighbors.

Lee was married to Minnie Waddy for almost fifty years—just one month shy. The daughter of Harry and Sarah Waddy, Minnie grew up in Safford, Alabama, and joined the Little Canaan Primitive Baptist Church. After leaving her hometown, she attended Alabama State University in Montgomery and obtained a Bachelor of Science degree in education. She was employed with the Perry County School System, where she diligently taught elementary school for thirty-seven years.

Minnie united with the Ward family church after marriage and was faithful in her Christian beliefs. She worked tirelessly in the church and the community, providing help for the elderly, young, or anyone who needed her assistance. After the church, her family was her priority.

- Shirley Ann Ward of Birmingham has a bachelor's degree in biology with a minor in chemistry from the University of Alabama at Tuscaloosa. She also holds a Bachelor of Science degree in medical technology from the University of Birmingham (UAB), an MBA, and a master's in public health from UAB. Shirley is currently employed at her alma mater in the field of medical technology, where she has worked for the past thirty-eight years.

- Tharone Brenford Ward of Atlanta, Georgia, is a graduate of the University of Alabama with a bachelor's degree in industrial arts and an associate's in mechanical engineering from Southern Polytechnical University in Marrietta, Georgia. Tharone taught for twenty-two years in the Atlanta public school system. He is the father of Tharone Lee Ward, the owner and operator of a truck driving business. The son is married to Nastassia, and they are the parents of Tharone Lucas, Tatiana, and Tyler Ward.

- Vinetta Yvette Ward lives in Charlotte, North Carolina. She received her Bachelor of Science degree in accounting from the University of Alabama at Tuscaloosa and her master's from Francis Marion University. Vinetta is a Certified Public Accountant, or CPA, licensed in North Carolina and in her home state of Alabama. She and husband Robert Harris are the proud parents of Robert Zachary and Grant Alexander Harris. Zachary recently graduated from the University of North Carolina with a BA in computer science.

  In reflecting on Lee's life, Dr. Ronald Henderson, co-author of *We Are the Wards!* stated that much of his cousin's success in farming and business was due to his ability to strategically navigate the racial-social-economic paradigm of the Deep South at that time. Ron credits Lee's keen awareness of "his place" and his profound understanding of the Southern white male's mentality. In that regard, Lee was very astute for the good of his farm, family, and future business.

Ron recalls a trip he made in 1975 from Gainesville, Florida, to Alabama with his mother, Mary Ella, and cousin Lucille Rutledge. During that visit, Lee took Ron with him to sell produce at several white establishments and finally to a market warehouse. As they drove in Lee's old, beat-up truck, he would turn on the air conditioning along the way, but as they got closer to the businesses, he would turn the AC off and roll down the windows in that steamy hot weather. Ron says this dance between turning the air on and off went on throughout the trip until he finally asked his cousin why he kept doing that, especially since Lee owned other air-conditioned vehicles, trucks, tractors and combines, and a late-model air-conditioned car. Lee responded, "They (the proverbial *the man*) don't need to know that I have AC in this old truck, and they don't need to know all that I have." The cousins then talked about what it was like living in the South and being able to prosper despite overt and covert hostility. At one point Lee laughed and said, in a matter-of-fact way, "We know some members of the Klan, including the mailman."

Their final stop that day was to a Winn-Dixie or a

Piggly Wiggly. Lee was all smiles, greeting everyone in sight. All the remaining bushels of okra and soybeans were unloaded. As they headed back home, Lee stated that every bushel had been sold that day and the white merchants expected him back to do more business on the next trip.

For nearly forty-four years, Ron has remembered his cousin's demeanor in dealing with the truck's appearance and its air conditioning, going to the rear of a restaurant to buy their lunch, and how jovial Lee was at every stop. He was impressed with how Lee conducted himself in ways that would not be perceived as a threat to white men. Ron says when he himself spoke to groups across the country or taught at colleges and universities, he often used Lee's humble, non-threatening demeanor and approach as examples of what nineteenth-century civil rights activist and sociologist W. E. B. Du Bois, author of *The Souls of Black Folk*, referred to as double consciousness. This concept of *two-ness* explains how people of color must always view themselves through the lens of a racist white society to "measure their own souls by the tape of a world that looks on in amused contempt and pity." To Ron, Lee had successfully balanced being both Negro and American "without the doors of opportunity being closed in his face," in the words of Du Bois.[8]

Scottie Mae Ward married Gus Davis from Hale County, Alabama, on December 22, 1957. She is Matt and Ella's great-granddaughter and the youngest of the children of Clark Sr. and Jerline Sanders, who died when Scottie was two years old; as a result, Scottie was raised by her paternal grandparents. But she had an image of her mother because, all her life, she was told she looked exactly like Jerline, who was a fair-skinned beauty with dark, twinkling eyes and a full head of thick, black hair. The few photographs Scottie has attest to their similarities and to her mother's natural beauty.

During Scottie's formative years in the early fifties, young ladies in the family were not allowed to walk home from church with the other boys and girls; they had to ride in the car with their strict parents. Sister said this was something that made her so mad because they were not allowed to have fun like the other children. And certainly, they could not date or go out alone with boys, so they either had to *court* on the front porch or go on dates with a chaperone. For Sister and Scottie, Ma Pearl was their chaperone.

Scottie gratefully admits that she was given the love and care that she needed to accomplish her goals in life. She earned

---

[8] W. E. B. Du Bois, *The Souls of Black Folk* (Chicago: A. C. McClurg & Co., 1903), 2–3.

a Bachelor of Arts degree from Alabama A&M University and spent most of her professional career teaching in the public schools of Cleveland, Ohio.

She and Gus are the parents of Kelvin and Derwin.

- Kelvin Davis, a successful over-the-road truck driver, is the father of Casey Frazier and grandfather of Ny'Jae Stephens

- Derwin Lydell Davis (April 3, 1961–January 4, 2019) had a natural aptitude for art, particularly sketches, and math, in which he received straight A's in school. After graduating from Shaker Heights High School in 1979, he attended Tri-C and Cleveland State University and completed his education at Central State University, graduating in 1985 with a degree in finance. Derwin's love of math translated into a career as a financial consultant and wealth manager with Morgan Stanley for more than twenty years, serving at one point as second vice president. Der or Double D, as he was called, and wife Felicia Plummer Davis are the parents of Mercedes (mother of Tristan Early) and Blake Ellington Davis.

  Everyone who loved Derwin were aware that *he knew the power of his Christian faith, understanding that suffering and death held their meaning in the resurrection of Jesus Christ.*

The Rev. John Lee Ward (born November 11, 1936) is the fifth of nine children and the youngest of three brothers. As such, he was spoiled by his sisters and protected by his brothers, all of which made him the loving, caring person he is today.

But his sister Dot says that no one would ever believe that, when he was growing up, John was scared at nighttime. He and his first cousin Douglas Cooke (son of Violet and William) went everywhere together, and because they did not drive, they walked many places. Everything would go well until darkness came. Then, Doug would have to walk John home every night, but sometimes not without playing tricks on his cousin.

A farmer for more than seventy years—he began farming at the age of ten—John raised chickens, turkeys, and cows and hunted rabbits to help supplement the family income. There was nothing too hard for him to do, and when his father, Clark Sr., died in 1960, he became the father figure so he could see that his mother, Pearl, whom he cherished, was well cared for. He worked day and night to provide for her and three of his sisters who were in college at the time. He later expanded his crops to include cotton, okra, and last, soybeans. John was also a cattle farmer.

For most of his life, and in the Ward tradition, John had one of the largest, most successful farms in Alabama, owning or leasing nearly fifteen hundred acres of land with a workforce of more than ten employees during his tenure as an entrepreneur. Considered a business farmer, he ran his farm like a corporation just as any other major farmer, Black or white. John purchased the biggest John Deere tractors and Gleaner combines that were manufactured, many of which were equipped with air conditioning, radios, and cassette tape players at the time.

In 1996–1997, John was featured in a documentary titled *The Forgotten Black Farmers in the South.* In it, a film crew from the University of Alabama shadowed John during a soybean planting and harvesting season. The film aired on Alabama Public Television for two years and told how, for decades, the USDA systematically discriminated against Black farmers, denying them access to loans, government-sponsored subsidies, and crop disaster relief while granting such loans and aid to white farmers. As a result, many Black farmers were forced out of business, losing their farms and homes; others died waiting for justice. In protest, in 1997, a caravan of Black farmers on tractors descended on USDA headquarters in Washington, DC to pressure the government for equality. Justice finally came on April 14, 1999, when a federal judge approved the settlement in the farmers' class-action suit and awarded the litigants $1.25 billion.[9]

John Lee Ward played an integral part in the farmers' fight for justice. However, his political activism began decades earlier when he was elected as one of the first two Black Perry County

---

[9] See details of the victory of Black farmers at https://www.blackenterprise. com/black-farmers-take-discrimination-protest-us-supreme-court/.

commissioners, along with Reese Billingsley, and served three consecutive four-year terms.

John was also a trailblazer! In 1977, as a Perry County commissioner, he and Commissioner Willie Sullivan motioned and seconded a proposed ordinance that Perry County would make the birthday of slain civil rights leader Dr. Martin Luther King Jr. a legal holiday, for which all county offices would close and all employees would have the day off. This observance became the first Dr. Martin Luther King Jr. holiday in the nation. The ordinance was passed and went into effect in 1978, celebrating January 15 of each year as an official holiday to commemorate the life of a great American hero. This historic action by Perry County commissioners occurred eight years before the United States Congress designated Dr. King's birthday a federal holiday in 1986. But it took another fourteen years before all fifty states observed the day. To honor his service, a road in Marion Junction was named the Reverend John Ward Road.

Through the years, John also served on the Agricultural Stabilization and Conservation Service (ASCS) board for eleven years. This board administered programs concerning farm products and agricultural conservation. John not only worked to save his own farm but also the livelihoods and lands of many of his constituents. He was also moderator of the Dallas County District Association for twenty-five years; second vice president of the Southwest State Convention; and first vice moderator of the Alabama Baptist Convention. His service and profound Baptist preaching abilities are recognized and respected by people around the country.

On November 24, 1963, John Lee Ward and Annie Mae Stephens were united in holy matrimony in a ceremony officiated by his father-in-law, Rev. Ezell F. Stephens. John's life partner, Annie Mae Stephens Ward, has supported her husband behind the scenes in all his endeavors, in farming, politics, and ministry.

He is the father of two daughters, grandfather of three, and great-grandfather of five:

- Dr. Wanda Katrice Ward (born August 23, 1967) holds a PhD in curriculum and instruction and higher education from Mississippi State University. She is currently a professor in the College of Education at Athens State University in Alabama. She serves as the adviser for the American Association of University Women's (AAUW) Student Organization on the campus. Dr. Humphrey is a published author and co-founder of Social Media Solutions, LLC. Her most recent work, *Help! Drowning in Social Media,* is a workbook for P–16 students that addresses social media etiquette, distracted driving, sexting, cyberbullying, loss of academically engaged time, and other perils that have the potential to ruin the lives and dreams of youth.

Her goal is for the workbook to be adopted by P–12 schools and colleges/universities around the world.

Passionate about real estate, Wanda became a licensed Alabama real estate agent in 2018. She is married to Levon Humphrey and has one daughter, Aleah Anjae.

- Dr. Stephanie Diane Haywood Bowlin, ED, PA, is a dean and associate professor at Western University of Health Sciences in Pomona, California. She is the mother of two, Ronnie Arnez Bowlin and Sheri Diane Bowlin, and grandmother of four: Maria Diane Bowlin, Sheri Dawn Bowlin, Shalie Diane Houston, and Xavier Arnez Houston.

Dorothy (Dot) Ward and Levi Reeves married and had two children, Tammie and Erwin. Dot graduated from Stillman College in Tuscaloosa, Alabama, and later earned a Master of Arts degree from San Francisco State University in California, with extended studies from the University of California.

Dot became a classroom teacher, reading resource specialist, and language arts curriculum supervisor for Richmond Unified School District, later known as West Contra Costa Unified School District California. She also served dutifully and in many capacities at the Church by the Side of the Road in Berkeley as a deacon, choir member, and Sunday School teacher.

- Erwin Lydell Reeves earned his bachelor's degree from Jackson State University in Jackson, Mississippi. He is currently employed with the Federal Deposit Insurance Corporation (FDIC) in San Francisco. He has been awarded the Star Award for contributions to the department and has volunteered in the community to assist low-income families in preparing their taxes, purchasing their first homes, and starting small businesses. A former senior vice president of Mechanics Bank in Richmond, California, Erwin received the George Carroll Award for community development activities in the West Contra Costa community.

- Tammie Reeves is married to the Rev. John Adams, pastor of the Elmhurst Presbyterian Church of Oakland, California. She has both a bachelor's and a master's in curriculum and instruction from California State University in Haywood. Tammie is continuing in the "family business," since both parents retired from teaching—her father, Levi, from Glenview Elementary School and her mother, Dorothy, from the Richmond public schools. Recognized in her district for becoming a National Board Certified Educator, Tammie has worked on the leadership team of the Oakland Unified School District for nearly twenty-five years. She is currently the principal of the Horace Mann Elementary School and serves as school improvement coach, supporting the instructional teacher leaders and principals in ten elementary schools in Elevation and Network 2.

Myrtis (Myrt) Ward and husband Frank Davis have one son, Christopher, and two grandsons, Omari and Jasai. An alumnus of Stillman College and the third of the Ward sisters to attend Stillman in Tuscaloosa, Alabama, Myrtis Ward Davis was an instructor in the Job Corps in Cleveland, Ohio. She was also employed as an executive assistant at Lincoln Electrical Company, one of the largest arc-welding companies in the world. In California, where she later relocated, she became an instructor at Laney College in Alameda, an executive assistant at Moore Business Farms, and an administrative assistant to the vice president of marketing at the Clorox Company in Oakland, California.

- Christopher Davis is a mechanic for Auto Truck Transport Trucking Company in Chico, California. He is the father of Omari, who graduated from St. George's High School in Newport, Rhode Island, and attends Hobart and William Smith Colleges in Geneva, New York. Chris's second son is Jasai Davis, an honor student at Pittsburg High School in Pittsburg, California.

Willie Jean Ward received a Bachelor of Arts degree from Stillman College. After graduation, Jean pursed a job assignment in Tuskegee, Alabama, where she met and married Richard Bruton Sr.; they had one son. Jean died at the age of twenty-six.

- Richard Bruton Jr. lives in Orlando, Florida, and is the owner of his own company, Small Business Fundz. It is a Christian-based company whose goal is to help the economy recover by helping business owners find working capital to grow or operate their businesses.

Walter Nevater (Vater) Ward married Charles Moore, and they are the parents of three: Charles Jr., Lester, and Vincent; they have ten grandchildren and eight great- grandchildren. Vater attended Booker T. Washington Business School in Birmingham, Alabama. She is a librarian at Birmingham City Library.

- Charles Moore Jr. attended Lawson Community College and has worked as an electrician for Alabama Power Company in Birmingham for over thirty years. He's married to Juanakee, and they are the parents of Demetris, Kevin, and Christana and grandparents of Kaden.

- Lester Moore and wife Jacqueline have six children—Terrell, Reginald, Michael, Jaden, Tiffany, and Briana. They have been blessed with seven grandchildren: Cloe, Tyree, Travon, Alicia, Amir, Kaleb, and Elijah. Lester has been employed for many years for Bruno's Warehouse and with UPS.

- Vincent Moore served in the US Marines and reserves and now works as an operation analyst for BBVA Compass Bank in Birmingham. He and wife Domini have two daughters: Jasmine, who graduated from the University of Alabama with a bachelor's in mechanical engineering, and Tiara, a high school student.

 **Arlene (Bae or Nin) Ward** was born in Browns, Alabama, on June 23, 1908, and died August 21, 1994, at age eighty-six. She married Paul Shears (May 5, 1902–June 28, 1998), a hometown boy. They had four children: twins Carl Lee and Delores Ann, Calvin Donald, and Jacqueline.

Arlene was born again and baptized at Woodlawn Baptist Church, where her father Rev. Otis Ward pastored. She initially attended elementary school in Uniontown; then, for the third through eleventh grades, she went to Lincoln High School, a private boarding school in Selma, Alabama. Arlene then ventured to Cleveland, Ohio, where she met and married Paul Shears and the two relocated to Cincinnati. There she enrolled in night school to receive her high school diploma to improve herself and set a standard for her children.

After Paul abandoned the family when the children were young, Arlene cleaned railroad train seats and worked as a domestic to feed her family. Refusing the help of her parents, who pleaded with her to send their four grandchildren to Alabama, Arlene worked hard to provide a clean, stable home, despite living in the Lincoln Courts Projects at 710 Clark Street. She sacrificed her life for theirs, always putting them first—perhaps even living vicariously through them because she was multi-gifted and could have been anything she wanted to be if not for her responsibilities as a mother of four and the times. However, she poured everything into her children and became their number-one cheerleader, sitting in the middle of the living room floor as they performed, telling jokes, singing, and dancing to her delight. *Arlene,* as they respectfully called her (not Mommy, Mom or Ma), accompanied her brood throughout Ohio and Kentucky, where they won musical and athletic contests. She encouraged them to excel in academics, sports, and creative pursuits, always reminding them *to never give any one power over them—but make that person earn it.*

Son Calvin recalls that Arlene would always point to a large-framed picture dated 1893 that depicted George Washington with other of America's Founding Fathers. It was titled "The Birth of Our Nation's Flag." Pointing, she would say, "No matter what's happening now, prepare yourself for when things get better."

In 1971, Arlene moved to Baltimore, Maryland, to be near her daughters. There she joined Wayland Baptist Church and enjoyed membership in the fuel club, the pastor's aide society, and the matrons. At Wayland, she was an adoptive mother and friend to many with whom she shared long, loving relationships.

Prim, proper, principled, and very vain, Arlene was one of a kind in her fashion-forward outfits with fancy, unusual touches. And her expensive, dramatic hats topped off the look—no church outfit was ever complete without a hat! As a fashion designer in her own right, Arlene delighted in sewing her daughters' clothes by hand and creating trend-setting hairstyles for them.

Described as stubborn, independent, and strong-willed (a trait she certainly inherited from her mother Carrie), she was blessed with the gift of discernment and would often say, "Oh, I can read you deep and wide." And that she could do because nothing ever escaped her eagle eye; Sonny, Doll, Donald, and Jaki knew that quite well.

Arlene Ward Shears knew herself better than anyone else, even when she stood alone, warts and all, boldly declaring her favorite expression: "I am myself."

Carl Lee (Sonny) Shears (April 17, 1936–March 7, 1979) married his first wife, Cynthia Jones of Columbus, Ohio, then was divorced and married Barbara Weaver, with whom he had a daughter named Lisa Arlene Shears, born October 26, 1968.

He was at best a modern-day Renaissance philosopher who probed knowledge and the future with fervor. A physicist, poet, prophet, publisher, professor, futurist, and jewelry maker, Carl Leemenzeer (the middle name he gave himself and preferred) marched to the beat of a different drummer. He had a thirst for learning and, in many ways, was a professional student, attending school from the age of four to forty-four, never missing a year. He attended the University of Cincinnati, Brigham Young University, Ohio State University, Washburn University, the University of London, and Oxford University. He earned his bachelor's degree in physics from Ohio State University and master's degree from Howard University; he later pursued doctoral studies at Howard, where he taught in the department of physics. At the time of his death in 1979, he was a professor of physics at the University of the District of Columbia.

Carl founded Nu Classic Publishers, which published scientific essays and books for many researchers, educators, and futurists in the Maryland-DC area. He was the author of more than fifteen books, among them *Countdown to Black Genocide,* and the author of a screenplay called *Sweet Jesus, Preacher Man.* Carl also published scientific journals often

147

written under the pen name of Saggitarus (*sic*). His writings remain a monument to the common man and woman because he was a seeker of justice for the oppressed.

Delores Ann (Doll, Dee) Shears, like her twin Carl, was a standout in school, where teachers at that time seated students by their IQs and their test scores. In each class, Sonny was always in the first seat and Doll in the second. This was remarkable since they attended predominantly white schools in Cincinnati with no Black teachers on staff. As a teenager, Doll was the first Black girl to sing on television in her hometown, winning many top prizes in singing contests and getting offers to perform in nightclubs. Of course, she had to decline because she was underage. Doll won other championship titles in track and broad jumping and as the *fastest Black typist in the city.* (It's true; they had typewriters at that time.)

After attending Morgan State College, now University, in Baltimore, she enjoyed a successful career teaching English in the public schools. After earning a Master of Arts degree from Antioch College in education and public administration, Doll enrolled in a dual University of Maryland program to earn a PhD and complete courses toward a law degree at the same time. After commuting the long distance from Baltimore to College Park, Maryland, she dropped out after a few weeks due to exhaustion.

Through the years, she created and co-hosted *Mata Means*

Woman, a talk show at WJZ-TV, the same station where Oprah Winfrey worked; directed the Management Development Center for the state of Maryland; and traveled the country conducting management seminars and giving motivational speeches. In 1984, as co-creator of Rebecca Robot and a family of robotic health-care givers, Doll took her creations to the World's Fair in New Orleans, entered Rebecca in the presidential primary in New Hampshire, and appeared with "her" on CBS's *Good Morning, America.* Her robotic family earned Doll a nomination for the National Medal of Technology at a prestigious banquet in the nation's capital.

For two years, Doll also researched cases filed in the Maryland state judicial system for litigants with extraordinary feuds to appear on the *Judge Mathis* TV show. One of her first cases to be broadcast by Judge Mathis was one involving a local university student whose boyfriend dumped her after she stopped taking care of him.

Arlene's older daughter is the author of five books, among which is the highly acclaimed *How to Get and Keep the Black Man in Spite of Women's Lib.* Doll says she has always tried to live a life of whimsy and reality at the same time.

- Roianne Pier Williams (born August 13, 1960) married Kevin Sullivan; their daughter is Keonne Sullivan-Johnson (who is married to Ronald D. Johnson). Roianne is a voracious reader, reading at least five books a week, and a tech whiz, having excelled in numerous high-tech training courses in high school and at Baltimore City Community College. Most of her adult career has been as an accounting specialist with DLA Piper, the fifth-largest law firm in the world. Roianne is a veteran of the United States Air Force and the Maryland National Guard.

• Rana Peri Williams (born January 7, 1964) and Clint Davis are the parents of Von Douglass, Evan, and Bianca Davis and grandparents of four. Rana has earned two associate's degrees, one each in humanities and paralegal studies, from the Midlands Technological College in Columbia, South Carolina. She also holds a Bachelor of Arts degree in human services from Columbia College. She has worked in the South Carolina House of Representatives, as a real estate agent, and as guardian ad litem—a court-appointed advocate for abused and neglected children. Rana currently works as a support manager of Choose Well, a South Carolina initiative aimed at reducing unintended pregnancies statewide, the first such effort in the state's history.

Rana is a passionate blogger, using the name *SUGnotes*.

Calvin Donald (CaShears) Shears's life is characterized by activism and stardom. At twelve years old, he and five friends integrated the Cincinnati Gardens, an all-white sports arena in his hometown. The friends wanted to play ice hockey in the segregated facility but were not received well by opposing players or their own teammates. They broke down barriers and played for five years, with Calvin becoming a star on the team. Along the way, he learned a valuable lesson from his white coach, who advised, "If you want to compete with the white boys, you must beat or compete with them at what they do, not because of their color."

In 1956, after graduating from Hughes High School, he enlisted in the US Army and played baseball at Fort Hood, Texas. Unknown to him, a scout for the Philadelphia Phillies baseball team took notice, advising the home office to sign Calvin and help get him an early release from the army. Mission accomplished—the Phillies' minor league office sent him to Montclair, New Jersey, where he stayed with Larry Doby, the first Black player in Major League Baseball. Calvin played for a year and a half in Elmira, New York, and Bakersfield, California (where he met his wife-to-be, Rita Crofton) until an arm injury cut short his career.

When he could no longer play baseball, Calvin considered a singing career and began perfecting his talents. Appearing in small clubs in Los Angeles, such as Tiki Island, Calvin then signed with a management company. He changed his name to **CaShears,** short for *Calvin* and *Shears*, and his career took off. CaShears performed in Playboy Clubs throughout the United

States and internationally in Australia, Argentina, Venezuela, England, Sweden, and the Caribbean. He often opened for such stars as Joan Rivers, Andy Williams, and Rodney Dangerfield. He became known as "an entertainer's entertainer" because of his rich, lyric, baritone voice; huge personality; and charismatic performances. He also headlined in a main room on the Las Vegas Strip.

However, it was during his 1980 South African tour with Grammy award winner Tina Turner that he experienced another epiphany. As CaShears visited an orphanage in Soweto, a female revolutionary challenged his views on apartheid, South Africa's state-sponsored system of discrimination against Black and colored Africans. It was against this repressive, racist institution that anti-apartheid revolutionary Nelson Rolihlahla Mandela fought and was jailed for twenty-seven years. (By the mighty hand of God, when apartheid fell, Nelson Mandela became the president of South Africa from 1994 to 1999.)

Declaring that her country did not need CaShears's tears or pity, the activist challenged him by asking, "Can you help?" So arrested by the question and her passion, the next day he gave thousands of dollars to the orphanage, along with truckloads of canned goods, clothes, shoes, hygiene items, and toys. He also purchased cassette players and over 150 cassette tapes and sent boxes of books for the twenty-eight children; this he continued to do for many, many years. Describing the birth of his humanitarian and activist spirit, CaShears says, "I was conceived in Soweto and born in South Africa."

When he returned stateside, he put his career on hold and devoted the next thirty years to championing social justice causes, working with welfare mothers and helping to diffuse tensions between rival Los Angeles gangs. For his humanitarian and civic work, CaShears has been honored by three US presidents: Ronald Reagan, Bill Clinton, and George H.W. Bush. He also received a letter of *thanks* from President Barack Obama, America's first African-American commander-in-chief.

CaShears was married to Rita Crofton from Bakersfield, California. She is the matriarch of the family and a registered nurse, homemaker, and devout Christian. Together, they have two daughters and one son.

- Leticia LaVette Crumpler is described as a semi-matriarch, a caregiver, and the glue that holds the family together. By training, Leticia is a nurse and a gifted poet and calligrapher. She and husband Derek live in Bakersfield.

- Demetrius (D'mitri) D'Vaughn Shears received his Master of Arts degree in education from the University of Phoenix in 2007. He currently works as a corrections officer in Delano, California. Multi-talented and gifted, D'mitri is a creative writer, animator, and cartoonist living in Bakersfield with wife Jenene Darrett Shears and their sons, Daniel, a student at Cal State University, and Christian, who is thirteen years old.

- DawnTina Shears earned a degree in education from the University of Phoenix and is employed with State Farm Insurance. She is politically astute yet family oriented. She and husband Rodney Skinner are the parents of fifteen-year-old Jaelyn, who is described as an all-round teenager—a computer genius, violinist, and ballerina.

Rev. Jacqueline (Jaki) Shears is the youngest of Arlene Ward and Paul Shears's four children. She was born in Cincinnati and graduated from Withrow High School. She then matriculated at Morgan State University, where she earned bachelor's and master's degrees in English. Within months of graduating, Jaki was appointed to be an assistant professor and would have remained at her alma mater if not for a providential encounter with a Baltimore broadcasting pioneer. In less than a week, she was lured away from MSU and hired by WMAR-TV as a reporter, then she worked at WRC-TV in Washington, DC and again in Baltimore at WJZ-TV as cohost of the award-winning talk show *City Line* for ten years.

Never satisfied to sit idly, Jaki then started her own advertising and public relations firm, Jaki Hall Enterprises Inc., or JHE, producing radio and television commercials for clients and publishing *The Black Pages*, a directory of Black businesses, and *Trés Chic*, a magazine for women with a French zest for life. After many years, she returned to teach at MSU or her *Fair Morgan*.

In 1985, however, Jaki realized that *only what you do for Christ will last*, and she gave her whole heart, mind, body, and strength to Christ and has not looked back. At the New Shiloh Baptist Church in Baltimore, she answered the heavenly call to ministry and was licensed to preach in 2004 by Drs. Harold A. Carter Sr. and Harold A. Carter Jr. She has also served as an English teacher in New Shiloh's Determined Biblical and Theological Institute and Bible study teacher in the Saturday Church School for more than a decade. She later earned a master's degree in theology from the Ecumenical Institute of St. Mary's Seminary and University, where she serves on the institute's alumni council.

From that time on, the Rev. Jaki Hall never gloried in her own accomplishments but rather has glorified the God of her salvation, witnessing Jesus Christ and serving hurting people under the power of the Holy Spirit. To accomplish this work, she founded The Daughters of Dorcas, Inc., a humanitarian ministry to the poor, homeless, elderly, and orphans, which is carried out through the ministry's adoption of two orphanages in Port-au-Prince, Haiti, just after the catastrophic 2010 earthquake. The ministry provides funding to the children from birth through college.

Jaki married Arthur Leo Hall; they had one daughter.

- Shana Roianne (Sha) Hall (married Edward Graves III) is the mother of Edward Alexander (Alex) Graves IV. Shana graduated in 1999 from Duke University with a Bachelor of Science degree in political science and public policy. While a student at Duke, Shana traveled to Belgium to participate in an international conference on conflict resolution at The Hague in Brussels. She is currently enrolled in the School of Continuing Studies at Georgetown University, pursuing an executive certificate in leadership coaching. For nearly twenty years, Shana has worked as a senior associate with PriceWaterhouseCooper, the world's largest consulting and professional advisement firm.

    In 2018, Shana founded Soma Triune, an executive leadership coaching firm designed to elevate the success skills of the total client: mind, body, and spirit.

Left to right, Lincoln "Buddy" Ward is shown with his cousin Bud Warren of Cleveland

Lincoln (Buddy) Ward (December 19,1910–May 27, 1939) fathered one son, Rev. Willie James Paige (January 7, 1935–June 23, 2006), who later became a minister in Cleveland, Ohio.

Thomas Jefferson (T or Unc) Ward (January 23, 1913–1996) was named after his maternal grandfather, Thomas Jefferson, who shared the same name as the third president of the United States and chief writer of the Declaration of Independence. "T," as he was called, married Candace Lapsley, with whom he had one daughter, Joyce Ann, who married Miller Pollard; they are the parents of Darren, Sonya, and Kai. After their divorce, Thomas married Clara Kelly.

Thomas was debonair and a sharp dresser. He always owned the latest-model cars and smoked fine, but stinky, cigars, according to his niece Jaki. He had an air of sophistication, a certain *je ne sais quoi* or an intangible, mysterious quality. From all accounts, he was a loner. And even though he kept mostly to himself, he always stayed close to another niece, Lucie, and her family. In fact, for more than twenty years, he lived in apartments owned by his grandnephew James McCall Jr. And by the grace of God, it was James, Lucie, and her family who took care of Unc during his declining years.

Unc was a long-standing member of the Bethlehem Baptist Church of Cincinnati and worked for decades for the Baldwin Piano Company.

According to the Ward family grapevine, at least three children were conceived outside of Otis and Carrie's marriage, including Hattie Mae Ward Turner of Los Angeles, CA; John (Johnnie) Ward of Uniontown, Alabama; and A.C. (We were unable to ascertain A.C.'s birth name or any other information.)

CHAPTER 8
ISABELLA (ISABELLE) WARD

I sabella Ward, born in Browns in May 1884, died on November 14, 1912. She married a farmer named Turner D. J. Bell (1857–June 6, 1919). The couple had two daughters: Ida Bell (1907-unknown) and Blanche Bell, who was born on June 23, 1912, and passed away on August 19, 1985.

ISABELLA'S DAUGHTERS AND THEIR CHILDREN

In 2014, the Detroit Family Reunion Committee accepted the challenge, along with other family members who had contributed during the 2012 reunion in Birmingham to ensure that a headstone would be placed at the site of the remains of our loved one Blanche Bell Caldwell, daughter of Isabella Ward

Bell and Turner Bell and granddaughter of Matt and Ella.

In July 2017, the headstone was set in place in Uniontown, Alabama, and the charge was met. A special *thank you* goes to Rev. Phillip White, Rev. John Lee Ward, Mrs. Annie Mae Ward, and the Detroit family committee that worked tirelessly to see this to fruition.

CHAPTER 9

LUDIE WARD

Ludie Ward was born in June 1881 and died March 3, 1942. He and his first wife, Rebecca Massey (1894–June 13, 1917), had four children: Albert, Roberta, Katie Mae, and Madison. After Rebecca died giving birth to their youngest child, Grandma Ella took care of the children until Ludie remarried.

He later married Viney Washington (1897–unknown), a member of the holiness church. One of Ludie's granddaughters, Roberta Williams Jackson (daughter of Katie Mae Ward) said, "Viney was good to us. I remember that she was beautiful and very shapely, with legs like Marilyn Monroe." Another granddaughter, Gloria Faye Thomas, recalls her mother, Roberta Ward, also saying that Viney, called Big Mama, was very kind and treated Ludie's children like her own. And when Big Mama moved to Saginaw, Michigan, after Ludie's death, it was said she often sent them boxes of beautiful dresses, skirts, and shirts that she herself had made.

Roberta Williams Jackson says her grandfather was good-looking and charismatic, with straight hair and the complexion of a *pecan*. Unlike his parents and many of his relatives, he was not a farmer but a self-proclaimed preacher who was often heard singing,

> *I Love the Lord.*
> *He heard my cry and pitied my every groan.*
> *Long as I live, and troubles rise,*
> *I'll hasten to His throne.*

Although Ludie did not pastor a church, Roberta says he held Bible study classes every Wednesday night on his front porch and in the front yard, with large crowds attending from all over. However, Gloria Faye's mother described Ludie as a lazy, jackleg preacher (a Southern term used to describe an untrained and unskilled minister) who didn't like to work. He was viewed as a "wannabe preacher" who believed that if he became a minister he could avoid working at the Birmingham steel plant. In fact, Roberta shared with her daughter that Ludie had once claimed that the part of the plant where he worked had burned down, causing him to lose his job. But when a co-worker went to check on him, the family learned the truth: the plant was still standing and operational. Believing he was too good looking and too good to work, Ludie chose instead to sit on the front porch and "eat peanuts all day."

Whether he was or was not a real preacher, Ludie Ward unfortunately suffered a stroke, becoming incapacitated and lingering for nearly two years. He died May 3, 1942, when his granddaughter Roberta Williams was thirteen years old. She remembers him lying in state in his living room in Ensley, Alabama, where his Bible students, neighbors, and others flocked to pay their respects. She says still others lined the road to watch the body go by.

LUDIE AND REBECCA'S FOUR CHILDREN AND THEIR CHILDREN

Albert Ward (1910–December 29, 1952) lived what Gloria Faye's mother described as a tragic yet sinful life. First, his son Albert Jr. lost both legs after being run over by a train and died in 1953 at the age of ten. Second, Albert was said to have had two wives and two sets of families, one with Cora Sally Willey (1905–1935) and another with Alice Ward (1914–1982). Albert later contracted tuberculosis and developed lung cancer. Broke from losing all his money gambling and as he lay dying from these debilitating diseases, it is said he became angry with God, screaming out that God had never done *nothing* for him. He would curse God, unlike the Old Testament figure Job, about whom it is written, "In all this did not Job sin with his lips" (Job 2:10). But Albert was heard berating God and saying, "I'm going to out-run death. I'm going to out-run death."

Sadly, he didn't run fast or far enough because he died in 1952.

With **Cora Willey**, he fathered **Mary Belle** (1925-2003) and **Mattie** (1926-1997). **Ludie** and **Alice Ward** had three children, **Ruth** (1932-), **Albert Jr.** (1933-1943), and **Sue** (1934-).

Roberta Ward (June 12, 1912—June 20, 1997) was "a diva before we ever used the term and before it became popular," says daughter Gloria Faye of Newport News, Virginia. Fashionable, proud, and stunning, Roberta was light skinned with long, straight hair. Although she always walked with her head held high, her daughter says her mother was not haughty or enamored with her exterior beauty but was truly a nice, peaceful woman who loved helping others, especially other women.

But Roberta's home life belied her demeanor because she had a difficult time, being abused mentally and psychologically by her husband, Roosevelt Williams (1906–1947). He worked for the L&M Railroad and unfortunately spent most of his money on himself to create an image of a dapper guy, dressed to the nines in the latest styles with his shoes always *spit* shined. His daughter says he spent money on clothes, but he did not take care of his children, leaving his wife Roberta to assume the responsibility and suffer through great tragedies with the deaths of three of their children. One of them, Roosevelt Jr., died after being hit by a train when he was three years old. Another child,

Rebecca, was so deformed that she died soon after birth. Still another son, Roy, died of rickets, a skeletal deformity resulting from a vitamin D deficiency.

To provide for her three remaining children, *Mudear*, as she was called, often worked two and three jobs at local hotels and cleaning private homes. She cleaned for others, but she also always kept her own children and home very clean. She was very particular. And although she and her children rented the house at 2026 Ensley Avenue in Ensley, Alabama, after Roosevelt Sr. left, none of the homeowners on the street would have ever known because Roberta kept the property and lawn just like everyone else. "Mudear explained, 'There's a reason to be poor, but there's no excuse to be dirty,'" declares Gloria Faye, who describes her mother as one of the cleanest women she has ever known.

Roberta Ward Williams, her daughter says, revered God and had a profound love for the Lord. She was a woman of great integrity who did not lose her integrity or her mind when Roosevelt abused her and abandoned the family but who lived ethically before her children, her family, and those she knew.

Charles Williams (August 31, 1931–November 1961) was the father of three children: Debra Ann Williams, Eric Williams, and Caroline Williams.

Gloria Faye Williams (born February 27, 1939) married John Ellis Thomas (born 1937), and from this union, they had seven children: Uwanna Donzella Thomas (1955); Sabrina Levetta Thomas (1957); John Ellis Thomas Jr. (1960); Edward Scherra Thomas (1962); Reginald Carl Thomas (1963); Ronald Earl Thomas (1964); and Krista Michelle Thomas (1966).

Jeannette Williams (born February 2, 1941) married John Kimbrough. They have three daughters: Jodi, Jerye, and Jan Kimbrough.

Katie Mae Ward (May 24, 1914–June 27, 1953) was a dark-skinned, heavyset woman who declared early on that "she wanted to marry a man lighter than her so that her children could be light."  Surely, she got her wish when she married Lloyd Williams (1911–1993), a light-skinned, good-looking man. But Katie Mae missed out in the area of her husband's character because Lloyd turned out to be a gambler, a womanizer, and a rolling stone, as shared by Gloria Faye's mother. Katie Mae was left to fend for herself and to do everything possible to provide for her family. Gloria Faye and her sister Jeanette visited their aunt every summer in Fairfield, and Gloria Faye says her aunt had an inferiority complex because of her looks and suffered in a marriage characterized by abuse and infidelity.

Lloyd Williams Jr. (March 16, 1932–May 25, 1970)

Roberta Williams (born July 17, 1933) married Madison Jackson (April 29, 1933–March 29, 1970). Together they had four children: Cathy Lavern Jackson (March 15, 1956–June 17, 2019), Madison Jackson Jr. (July 7, 1957–July 30, 1975), Alexander V. Jackson (January 27, 1959–September 22, 1966), and Rowchelle Jackson (born September 7, 1963).

Roberta's second husband was Earnest V. L. Landrum Jr. (May 9, 1932–July 5, 1986). Their children were Lance L. Landrum (1951–2015) and Earnest V. Landrum III (born 1952).

Clarence Williams (born January 6, 1935)

Madison (Matt) Ward, born in 1917 in Fairfield, was named after his grandfather and our patriarch. He and Dee Williams lived together for many years but never married. In fact, he never married anyone but had many, many women who took care of him. He lived what Roberta Ward described as a despicable lifestyle as well. Light skinned and good looking, like his father Ludie and brother Albert, Madison also disdained having to work for a living. His cousin Roberta said that Madison worked to party and that money only meant good times with lots of riotous living and drinking. Because he lacked scruples and foundational principles, at one point in his life, someone ambushed and shot him, but he survived. As a result, he developed a limp that lasted until he died violently in 1955 at the age of thirty-eight. Town gossip has it that he was poisoned, perhaps by one of his lovers even though no autopsy was performed to ascertain the cause of death nor was a perpetrator ever identified.

The funeral, it is said, became a "four-ring circus" when two women, each claiming to be his *woman*, began yanking Matt's casket back and forth and jerking the body from side to side, nearly throwing it to the floor. It was no better afterward, says Gloria Faye, when two other women got into a fight at the graveside.

CHAPTER 10

WILLIAM (BILL) WARD

William (Bill) Ward, who was born June 16, 1889, and died September 23, 1965, in Dallas County, married Chaney Fields (1893–1942) and had two boys, Cleophus and Eugene, and one daughter, Bessie Mae. At least one of the children, if not all, obtained a college degree and became the first schoolteachers in the Ward family. After the death of Chaney, William, at age fifty-five years, married Elizabeth Lyles, a thirty-eight-year-old widow, and the two settled in Ensley.

He was a brick mason by trade and became quite successful. His niece Gloria Faye, who with her sister Jeanette visited their Uncle Bill often, says he owned a large home with a roomy, welcoming foyer; the home had white front pillars and a great wrap-around porch. At opposite ends were two big swings where sometimes Uncle Bill's grandchildren would swing at one end with Gloria Faye and her sister at the other. The house sat in the middle of a well-manicured lawn, replete with pear and fig trees.

WILLIAM AND CHANEY'S CHILDREN AND THEIR CHILDREN

Cleophus Raymond Ward (born August 9, 1909–April 7, 1973) was a teacher who later enlisted in the US Army at Fort Benning, Georgia, during World War II. He later married Gussie B. Ward and had twin boys named Robert and Raymond (born 1934).

Eugene (Gene) Ward (1912–August 1972) owned a coal yard and had three sons.

Bessie Mae Ward was born on September 15, 1914 and died in 1988. She married Robert Jackson and had two daughters: Rustine Jackson and Etta Jean Jackson.

CHAPTER 11

GOLDEN WARD

Golden Ward (August 16, 1894–December 23, 1938) married Eugenia Mason and settled in Fairfield, Alabama, where they raised their three children, Leocie, Lucille, and James Golden—all of whom completed high school.

Eugenia Mason Ward and Golden, a farmer, were described as loving, kind, and hard working. They were a religious, Spirit-filled family who were members of the Church of Christ.

GOLDEN AND EUGENIA'S CHILDREN AND THEIR CHILDREN

Leocie (Top) Ward married Charles Nelson of Macon, Georgia. From this union, eleven children were born: Charles Jr., Paul, Melvin, Donald, Shirley, Eugene, Gwendolyn, Frederick, Tyrone, Nathan, and Terry. Nearly all their offspring left Fairfield, settling in other cities in Alabama and Georgia or traveling to Detroit and Cleveland during what was called the Great Migration (1910–1940 and 1940–1970), the mass exodus of African Americans from the South to northern or midwestern cities, fleeing oppression and seeking better job or educational opportunities. Most of the Nelsons sought employment in the service field, with humanitarian or social work skills or some form of business administration.

Leocie, according to her daughter Shirley Nelson Humphries, was always a happy person with a contagious smile and a huge love for her family and God. Shirley says her mother was caring, comforting, sharing, mentoring, and a great provider. Shirley says she was also an excellent cook; among her favorite dishes was stuffed cabbage. Leocie attended nursing school and later worked at Estee's Nursing Home for ten years.

Her husband Charles, who completed high school, is said to have worked all the time as a laborer and a tailor. Possessing a great business mind, he was an excellent financial planner and money manager. He provided well for his family's financial security, becoming their rock and safety net. Besides loving his wife and eleven children, Charles Nelson had an avid love for God.

Charles Nelson Jr. (1940–July 28, 1944)

Elder Paul Nelson (September 28, 1942) served twenty-one years in the air force, retiring as a captain. He was one of two individuals responsible for building and completing the Central Arizona Project (CAP) to bring water from the Colorado River into central and southern Arizona. He also became one of the first Elders to be sworn in at Azusa World Ministries in 1998.

He and wife Georgia Nelson, now deceased, had three children:

- Pastor Eric West Nelson, who is married to Vivian West (parents of Tristan Paul, Michael Ray and Eric Paul), retired from the State of California, Department of Corrections. He pastors the United in Christ Ministries Church in Bakersfield, California.

- Paul Nelson Jr. was married to the late Prudence Nelson. He is the father of Paul Anthony III, Zachary, and Brandon. Paul Jr., who has his own business called P&P One Care; it is a carpet cleaning and handyman service. He is also a Coffee News and U-Haul franchisee. He resides in Phoenix, Arizona.

- Yvonne Nelson and husband Derek Johansen, a software engineer, live in Denver, Colorado, with their son Samuel and daughter Sarah. Yvonne, a graduate of Arizona State University, is a systems engineer in the aerospace and avionics field. She formerly worked for the Intel Corporation.

Melvin (Bachie) Nelson (August 12, 1944–February 4, 1999), son of Leocie Ward Nelson and Charles Nelson, was born in Fairfield. He gave his life to Christ early and served faithfully at the Cairo Church of Christ (Roosevelt City) until his health declined. He married Deborah and they had two children, a son Reginald and a daughter Jeanette, who lives in Germany.

Elder Donald Nelson (born March 19, 1946) married Georgia Pritchett, with whom he had two daughters: Aleisha Nelson, who retired from the US Air Force, and Donnese S. Nelson, a radio/television personality. Both reside in the Charlotte, North Carolina area. Aleisha and husband Chris Thompson have two daughters, Kaja and Aliya Thompson.

Donald later married Annie Williams with whom he fathered a son Donnell Nelson (father of Donnell, Jr., affectionately known as *Little Donnell*), in addition to an existing son, Andre Williams, father of daughter Andrea.

Donald and Annie settled in Cleveland, Ohio, where Donald became the first Elder of the University Church of Christ in 2017.

Shirley (Shirl) Nelson married Tommie Humphries. Together, they had three children, Deandre Michelle, Deidre Renee, and Melanie Trenise.

- Deandre Michelle is married to Rufus Hudson; they are the parents of daughter Kyra Denae Hudson, in addition to another daughter, Ashlee Hudson, and a son, Dierré Hudson. Michelle works as a front office coordinator for a local physician.

- Deidre Renee is the senior manager for microbiology at Fareva Pharmaceuticals (VA) and has one daughter, Kaela LeAnne Howell.

- Melanie Trenise and husband Roger Allen Sharp are the parents of Denae Lena Trenise Sharp and son Devin Allen Lee Sharp. Melanie serves as the center manager for the Program for All-Inclusive Care of the Elderly or PACE. Roger is a support staff member at Detroit Metropolitan Airport.

Eugene (Gene) Nelson is a retired supervisor for a government contractor. While actively working, he received recognition as employee of the year and an all-expense-paid trip to Florida. Eugene currently serves as a trustee for Northwest Church of Christ (Detroit). He and wife Sandra have two daughters, Shernita Darnelle (deceased October 13, 1999) and LaTonya Rochelle Nelson. LaTonya is the mother of Trayvon Martin (not the Trayvon Martin who was killed in Florida) and Tyler Demarlon Nichels.

Gwendolyn (Wee Wee/Weekie) Nelson (February 2, 1951–January 21, 2014) was the seventh of eleven children born to the late Charles and Leocie Nelson in Fairfield. Creative, imaginative, talkative, friendly, and humorous, Gwen was always busy doing something, even as a child. According to family, no one could out-wit, out-talk, or out-plan her on special events; she was a very classy lady with extraordinary talents, one who cared for and helped others. She was gifted with a photographic memory and extraordinary writing skills.

Gwen confessed Christ as a child at Cairo City Church of Christ (known today as Roosevelt City Church of Christ). She loved the Lord and was instrumental in getting her husband Arnold Abraham and sister-in-law Annice Belin to become members of the Church of Christ. She enjoyed sharing the sermons of Minister Dallas A. Walker Jr. with her parents and other out-of-town relatives, and each Sunday, the family would exchange sermon notes for fun.

In 1992, Gwen met and married Arnold in what can be called a match made in heaven. He lovingly described their meeting and union this way:

> From the day I met you, I knew you were something special, someone to call mine. From the day I met you, you were always first. Whatever you wanted, I would go through any and everything to get. You would come before anything I ever wanted because your happiness was all I wanted. From our fun times spent on cruises and road trips to blessing me with our "miracle baby," Ashlee, you completed me and gave me everything I needed.

In high school, "Weekie" was chosen to be the news reporter at Wenonah High, which gave her a spot on radio station WJLD to report school news. After graduation, she moved to Detroit, where she worked as a business consultant for Michigan Bell Telephone Company, General Motors EDS, Ford Motor Company, and the City of Detroit.

She loved school and was very passionate about education. To her credit, she earned an associate's degree from Wayne County Community College (June 1980), a master's degree from the University of Detroit-Mercy (May 2001), and a second master's from Madonna University in project management (May 2012).

- Ashlee Abraham, called *a miracle child* by her parents, is a native of Detroit and was an outstanding track and field athlete in high school. She received a scholarship to Eastern Michigan University, where she set the Mid-America Conference record for the sixty-meter dash. Ashlee later transferred to Ohio State University and graduated in 2014. Her accomplishments in track and field include becoming a Big Ten champion three times and an NCAA All-American five times.

  Ashlee is currently employed as a financial literacy coordinator at Impact Community Action in Columbus, Ohio.

Frederick (Prima) Nelson (August 28, 1952–May 19, 1986) married Barbara; they were the parents of three daughters: Christina, Stephanie, and Pamela. Upon graduating from high school in 1970, he enlisted in the US Army and served his country proudly for fourteen years until his health failed, forcing him to retire. But even with failing health, Fred continued to spread the Word of God through studies and Bible sessions with family and friends. Promoting the need for love, togetherness, and unity, Fred's last words were, "Thank you, Jesus, for everything."

Tyrone (Tye) Nathan Nelson married Vernell Barrow-Nelson (now deceased) and lives in Birmingham. His children from a previous relationship are Jonathan Finch and Latonya Smith. Tyrone retired from Homewood Parks and Recreation after serving many years as a skilled laborer. He is a member of the Roosevelt City Church of Christ.

Nathan (Na) Nelson and wife Shirley have three sons and a daughter: Xavier, Stanton, Nijah Pierre, and Shana Nelson. Nathan retired as a laborer for a local industry; he is on the deacon board of the Roosevelt City Church of Christ in Alabama.

- Xavier Nelson provides legal services in Alabama.

- Stanton Nelson is employed as a security engineer at Best Buy.

- Nijah Nelson, who works as a machine operator at a Georgia printing company, is married to Shetia Nelson, with whom he has two sons and one daughter: Zyre Reid, Tytus Prince, and Nyana Ayana.

- Shana Nelson, like her mother Shirley, is a registered nurse.

Terry (Moon) Nelson, PhD, is the founder and chief executive officer (CEO) of New Generation Education Solutions, LLC, a full-service consultancy dedicated to improving teaching and learning and to developing programs to increase equity, access, and excellence. He recently served as director of teaching and learning for a local school district, where he successfully led schools and district offices through AdvancED accreditation procedures to complement his previous service as chairperson on several accreditation teams. As executive director for a state regional educational service agency, Terry provided leadership on major initiatives in 120 schools, which served approximately ninety thousand students.

Throughout his professional career, Dr. Nelson has collaborated with educators, legislators, businesses, and community-based organizations, providing leadership and support in the areas of workforce, policy and organizational development and implementation, strategic planning, diversity management, and stakeholder engagement. Among his many achievements, he held memberships on numerous task forces and committees, including serving as a member of Envision Prince George's County, a participant in the District Heights Closing the Achievement Gap Community Conversation, a peer reviewer for US Department of Education grants, and a member of the Maryland State Department of Education Committee of Practitioners. Dr. Terry Nelson was also the recipient of the Dr. Isaiah Reid Distinguished Leadership Award from South Carolina State University for outstanding leadership and services to improve public schools in Georgia, North Carolina, and South Carolina.

He received his doctorate and educational specialist degrees in education administration from South Carolina State University, his master's degree in higher education administration from Southern Illinois University, and his bachelor's in health education from Mississippi Valley State University. He currently lives in Martinez, Georgia.

Terry married Wanda L. Joiner (deceased), and they had four children: Chandra, Zachary, Terrilyn, and Tevin.

- Chandra Cox works as a service delivery consultant and is the mother of three daughters: Martavia Corley (mother of Isaiah Ali Sumpter and Chrislyn Lee Sumpter); Zantiya Luckett (mother of Masigah Jamaal

Surry, King Akeem Hayes, and Layla Rain Patrice Hayes); and NaChazney Cooper, who lives in Savannah, Georgia, and is majoring in forensic accounting at a local college.

- Zachary Nelson has a master's degree in music education and serves as assistant band director at his former high school. He is the father of Travis Dean Nelson and Madison Elyse Nelson.

- Terrilyn Nelson, a registered nurse at a major research hospital in Georgia, is married to Dustin Daniels, and they are the parents of Braylen Daniels and Ayden Daniels. Dustin has an MBA and is a budget analyst for Savannah River Nuclear Facility in Aiken, South Carolina.

- Tevin Nelson has a Bachelor of Science degree in mass communication and public relations from Bowie State University in Bowie, Maryland, and a master's in public administration, also from Bowie State. Tevin is employed by the Lockheed Martin Corporation as an asset manager.

Lucille (Honey) Ward (April 2, 1920– February 7, 1976) was born in Fairfield. She accomplished a rare achievement for a colored woman during that era— she graduated from high school, took

classes at Booker T. Washington Business School, and became a teacher in the Sprott County (now known as Perry County) public school system.

Lucille confessed Christ as a child and joined the First Baptist Church of Fairfield, where she was a faithful member until, in 1955, she followed her husband of seventeen years, Luther Rutledge, in relocating to Detroit. Lucille then joined People's Community Church and served as a faithful Sunday School teacher, a member of the courtesy club and the April club, and an active member of the 2600–2700 Glendale block club.

She and Luther, known as Big Luke, had two daughters, Marjorie and Geraldine, and three sons, Golden Luther, Carl, and Arthur.

Marjorie Dean (Sugar) Rutledge completed high school and business college with a major in accounting. She was a supervisor of accounting in a bank and retired in 1996. Marjorie and Henry Brown, now deceased, had two sons

- Kelvin Henry Brown is the father of Tessalonia Brown Westbrook (Robert) and grandfather of Xavier Norman Westbrook.

- Kenneth Henry Brown is the father of Dantrell Savage and Daijivon Brown.

Golden Luther (Bro or Broman) Rutledge (April 20, 1940– January 20, 1982) attended public schools in Alabama but completed high school in Michigan. After graduation, he served honorably in the US Army; he was later employed at the Chrysler Stamping Plant in Detroit. Bro and wife Sallie were the parents of Tonya Trinace Rutledge, grandparents of Jonah Swaggerty, and great-grandparents of Nasir Swaggerty.

Carl Edward Rutledge graduated from a high school in Detroit and served in the US Army. After receiving an honorable discharge, Carl worked in the auto industry until his retirement.

Arthur Milton (Tinnie Boy) Rutledge and wife Annie are the parents of two: Jeffrey Rutledge and Cindy Sohio Nix, the mother of Toni Jones.

Geraldine (Geri) Rutledge made history in 1969 when she became the first African American to graduate from the nursing program of Madonna University. Ironically, she then helped the same program achieve its accreditation. Geri's nursing career is broad and full of superlatives. Among the many hospitals where she was on staff are North Detroit General Hospital as a charge nurse and operating room supervisor; the predominantly Black Kirwood Hospital as charge nurse; and the Surgical Centers for Botsford (now Beaumont) Hospital, as part of the team that opened it. When she suffered a job-related injury, she began working at Hospice of Michigan, Home Care, and as a case worker for Aetna of Michigan.

Humanitarian and volunteer service has been integral to Geraldine's life. Under the auspices of the American Red Cross, she participated in the Hurricane Katrina Disaster Relief Campaign. This category 5 hurricane hit America's Gulf Coast on August 29, 2005, flooding the region and devastating cities from Florida to Louisiana; by the National Hurricane Center's count, an estimated thirteen hundred to eighteen hundred people were killed and $125 billion in property destroyed, with thousands of Gulf Coast residents left homeless. Geri traveled to Dallas to help bring residents who had been evacuated from New Orleans and other cities to safety in Detroit. She also volunteered as a CPR educator in churches, and for more than twenty-five years, Geri served as a camp nurse.

Her professional credentials include time as president of

the Association of Operating Room Nurses (AORN) and Operating Room Supervisors and Managers. For her years of sterling service to residents, Geraldine Rutledge was awarded the State of Michigan Special Citizen Award.

Geri was married to Leon Morehead and then to Frank Johnson.

- Rev. Leon B. Morehead is a graduate of Great Lakes Christian College with a degree in family life education and of Rochester College with a degree in biblical studies. Leon has worked with emotionally impaired children for more than twenty years. Since being licensed in May 2007 as a minister of the gospel of Jesus Christ, he has served the Greater New Mount Moriah Baptist Church—as youth minister in 2008, interim youth director in 2015, and executive minister since 2016.

  He and wife Maleika Pritchett are the proud parents of Leon B. (LJ) Morehead Jr. and Moriah P. Morehead

- Francyine Johnson earned a Bachelor of Science degree in interdisciplinary studies of social sciences from Michigan State University (MSU). She recently received an award for ten years of service with Blue Cross Blue Shield of Michigan.

James Golden (Sweetman) Ward (February 7, 1924–January 25, 2003), the youngest of three, was  born in Jefferson County, Alabama. He attended Fairfield Industrial High School. He later served as a sergeant in the US Army and was awarded the European–African–Middle Eastern Service Medal. James was a devoted member of the First Baptist Church of Fairfield, where he was appointed church clerk, chairman and financial chairman of the deacon board, trustee, and chairman of the baptismal committee, and he served in many other capacities. He was also a faithful member of the Fairfield Spirituals Gospel Singers.

For years, he was the financial secretary of the local union 1700 of the USWA-CIO and union representative for the United Steelworkers of America. James was notably a presenter at the nationally televised Constitutional Convention for the union in Las Vegas, Nevada.

Sweetman, as he was called, was married to Thelma Butts and had five children: Denise, Jacqueline, Gloria, Nadine, and Michael.

Denise Ward was born in Fairfield to James Golden and Thelma Ward and died on November 2, 1994. After completing high school in her hometown, she relocated to Los Angeles, California. Denise was an advocate in South Central LA, where she counseled youth, worked with family reunification projects, and networked with many community service leaders. She was described as a beautiful daughter, true sister, wonderful mother, loving companion, and friend to many. She loved life and was passionately devoted to her family, especially to her son Erik. And when she walked into a room, it was said, she changed the atmosphere. Giving of herself and her time didn't faze her; it only made her laugh. God's mercy was given to her daily in life, and great grace abided with her in death. In the words of Romans 8:38–39:

> *For I am persuaded, that neither death, nor life, nor angels, nor principalities, nor powers, nor things present, nor things to come, nor height, nor depth, nor any other creature, shall be able to separate us from the love of God, which is in Christ Jesus our Lord.*

Jacqueline (Jackie) Ward graduated from Fairfield Industrial High School in Alabama and entered the workforce in retail, housekeeping, and medical services.

She is the mother of two sons, Donnie and Kenton Smith and one daughter Amber Smith and proud grandmother of eight.

Rev. Gloria Ward Wyatt graduated from Fairfield Industrial High School in Fairfield, Alabama. Currently, she serves as president of the Leadership Team for Aglow International—Michigan Southeast Area Region. Gloria is a speaker, encourager, and singer and has been blessed to travel extensively throughout the United States and overseas on missionary and evangelistic tours, living out the Great Commission in Matthew 28:19: "Go ye therefore, and teach all nations, baptizing them in the name of the Father, and of the Son, and of the Holy Ghost."

Gloria is the mother of four: Felecia Wyatt McNeal, Darian, JoVon and Quintel Wyatt; grandmother of eleven, and great-grandmother of three.

Michael (Mike) Ward, was born on November 12, 1956, in Fairfield, where he joined First Baptist Church and graduated from Fairfield High School. He was a lover of nature and enjoyed gardening and fishing; he would take his boat out in the water and later share whatever he caught with everyone. He was considered a jack-of-all-trades and was self-taught in many skills, including repairing cars, doing carpentry work, and playing the guitar. Mike was at one point a member of the MINT Band and played lead guitar for the music group the Soul Controllers. He was also a studio guitarist for many artists and was lead guitarist in 1979 on the popular disco song "Ring My Bell" by Anita Ward. (We're not able to ascertain whether Ms. Ward is related to our family, but the idea is intriguing!)

- DeAqua Denise Hall of Fairfield, Alabama

- Miguel Terrence Hayes of Atlanta, Georgia

- Trimese Michelle Ward of Atlanta, Georgia

Nadine Ward is the youngest of James and Thelma's five children. After high school, Nadine attended Alabama A&M University in Huntsville, earning her bachelor's and master's degrees in psychological social work. She began her career in the mental health field in Tuscaloosa but later moved to Los Angeles, California, to continue her career at Torrance Memorial Hospital. Nadine was promoted to the position of chief operating officer (COO) at Vital Care Network. Health reasons caused Nadine to take an early retirement and move back to Birmingham with family, whom she loves and adores.

CHAPTER 12

DAVIS WARD

December 25, 1895–April 10, 1976

---

[10] There is disagreement between the authors on including Davis Ward as a son of Matt and Ella because several census reports list conflicting information that has not been reconciled.

CHAPTER 13

JOHN WARD

John Ward,[11] born in October 1896 in Browns, Alabama, is believed to be the youngest son of Matt and Ella. John married Susie Sanders in Perry County. She was one of the five children of Jimmie and Hannah Sanders, slaves and sharecroppers from Virginia who were later sold to a slaveholder in Selma. Jimmie and Hannah migrated to Uniontown, where their daughter Susie met and married our relative John Ward. To this union, five children were born: Susie Ward (Davis), John Ward Jr., Mary Ward (Hudson), Maggie Ward (Clark); and Bertha Ward, who married Joe Earl Jackson in Perry County, then migrated to Fairfield,

---

[11] There is disagreement between the authors on including John Ward as a son of Matt and Ella because several census reports list conflicting information that has not been reconciled.

Alabama. There they raised their eight children: Rosa, Samuel, Henry, Joe Earl Jr., Mozelle, Lelia, Bertha Mae, and Doris.

John and Susie lived in Marion, Alabama, until John's death on April 10, 1976. Afterward, Susie sold most of their possessions and moved to Birmingham, where she settled with her children until her death.

CHAPTER 14

LAURA WARD

Laura was born in August 1898 in Browns, Alabama, and died July 21, 1923. The youngest of Matt and Ella's seven children, she married Herbert Childs (October 18, 1893–September 21, 1967) from Perry County. The couple had two daughters, Mary Ella and Ethel Ruby.

Because Laura died at age twenty-four, when her girls were young, very little is known about her life.

More is known about Herbert, who relocated to Detroit and found work as a laborer, constructing the tunnel to Canada. He later worked on the assembly line at the General Motors (GM) Fisher Body Plant. Interestingly, however, work opportunities were not the primary reason for his move. According to his daughters Mary Ella and Ruby, Herbert got into an altercation with a policeman in Phoenix, Alabama; got the better of the officer; and took his gun and brass knuckles. His stepdaughter Minnie Mae reports that in order to get out of town fast, he hopped a freight train to Detroit, taking with him the items he confiscated from the officer.

Herbert Childs, standing six feet five inches tall, is described as good looking and a sharp dresser. The most prominent information about him was  his full participation in the nightlife of Black Bottom/ Paradise Valley, where most of the colored population of Detroit resided. He was active in what is known as a shadow society or subculture of the majority community that involved clubbing, partying, and gambling. Black Bottom had its own colored-owned nightclubs, theaters, and businesses because it was prohibited from interacting with Caucasian society, and Herbert Childs enjoyed it to the fullest.

Grandson Ronald (son of Mary Ella) remembers

living upstairs from his grandfather on Hasting Street until he was about four years old and visiting him often during his later years.

He recalls that his grandad always listened to baseball games while resting. At that time, his favorite team was the Cleveland Indians because it was the first American League team with Black players—Larry Doby, Satchel Paige, Minnie Minoso, and others. Also, Herbert and his second wife, Johnnie Mae, often hosted parties where food was sold and money wagered on games of chance.

LAURA AND HERBERT'S DAUGHTERS AND THEIR CHILDREN

Mary Ella (Sis) Childs (March 28, 1920–May 30, 2010) was one of two daughters born to Laura Ward and Herbert Childs in Bessemer,  Alabama. Mary Ella was raised by Grandma Ella after her mother died when she was five years old. She received her early education, to about the seventh grade, in Alabama and then moved to Detroit at the age of twenty to seek employment and be near her father.

She lived with her father until she married Charles Henderson in 1942. The son of a Pullman porter, Charles and his family moved around, from Carlisle, Kentucky, to Cincinnati to Grand Rapids and finally to Detroit, where he married Mary Ella. They had two sons, Ronald and Bernard, and one daughter, Frankie. Charles attended the Chrysler Engineering program and worked at Dodge Main Auto Plant Foundry. He also worked part-time for McFall's Funeral Home in Detroit. Ron remembers that his dad was a handy man who could repair cars, appliances, washing machines, watches, and just about everything else. Beyond this, he recalls several fishing trips to Canada with his father but very little else because he did not see him often after his parents divorced in 1947. Charles Henderson passed away on May 5, 1962, at the age of fifty-nine.

After her divorce, Mary Ella married Henry McCormick Kirkland (October 20, 1913–December 15, 1981), who was born and raised in Ensley, Alabama, but attended Parker High School in Birmingham. After being honorably discharged as a corporal from the US Army, Henry settled in Detroit and was employed by Indian Village Cleaners as a presser for more than thirty-two years. In fact, according to his son Ronald, he worked nonstop, often holding down two or three jobs at the same time. While many families in Detroit experienced periods of their fathers' not working in auto plants due to model changeovers and layoffs, Henry and Mary Ella's family never felt the crush of unemployment because he was a *workaholic* who wanted to provide economic security for his family.

Together, he and Mary Ella had six children—four sons and two daughters, all of whom were born and raised in Detroit. The blended family was active in Eastern Star Missionary Baptist Church (renamed Triumphant Life Christian Church) and later in Faith Tabernacle Church in Highland Park, where Henry served as a deacon. They sang in the choirs, attended Bible studies, and participated in holiday programs. Their home on Cameron Street in Highland Park was a gathering place, not just for their large family but also for the neighborhood kids, even those who were not welcomed in many other homes because Mary Ella treated every child the same and fed everyone who sat at her table.

During World War II, Mary Ella worked in an

industrial plant, but after the births of her children, most of her time was spent in the home, with sporadic domestic work in hotels and private homes. During the latter part of her life, she worked as a pastry chef at a monastery in Royal Oak, where Roman Catholic priest Father Charles Coughlin resided. This controversial cleric hosted a weekly radio show on which he was alleged to have espoused anti-Semitic views to an estimated thirty million listeners.

Mary Ella served with dignity at the Royal Oak Monastery and everywhere else she worked. Tall, with a medium brown complexion, and well-built, she was described as fashionable, with matching outfits and hats for every season and occasion. Ron remembers that one of the treats of his professional life was when he went shopping with his mother to pick out his topcoats, ties, suits, and other items because she had such an eye for fashion. A no-nonsense disciplinarian, she was very neat and clean. In addition, she was a stickler for schoolwork, took seriously her children's education, and was active in the Thompson Elementary School Parent Teacher Association. She even sang in the parent singing group called the Musical Moms.

However, it was his mother's emphasis on family—both nuclear and extended—that knitted her children to one another and to the Wards. This family-first mantra has been a consistent for co-author Ronald Henderson, who found during his years of professional travel that he would meet many family members by introducing himself simply by repeating what his mom told him: "Just say you're Mary Ella's oldest son."

Mary Ella's religion and service for the Lord were always a priority in her life. She joined Eastern Star Missionary Baptist Church in 1964, serving as president of the choir and as an usher. Twenty-two years later, she united with Mount Hebron Baptist Church, where she was a faithful member of the nurses' guild.

A mother, a grandmother, a great-grandmother (affectionately called GG), an auntie, a cousin, a friend—but above all, Mary Ella was a servant and child of the Most High God.

After Mary Ella Kirkland's death in 2010, her daughter Retta Zeigler had an idea that resonated with her siblings—to establish a scholarship in their mother's name at her church, Mount Hebron Missionary Baptist

Church in Detroit, Michigan, to commemorate Mary Ella's emphasis on education. The program is held on Baccalaureate Sunday, the fourth Sunday in June every year. To date, since the first service in June 2011, the Mary Ella Kirkland Scholarship program has awarded over sixteen thousand dollars in assistance to sixteen graduating high school students.

Ronald D. (Professor or Ron) Henderson, PhD, co-author of *We Are the Wards!* earned his bachelor's and master's degrees from Wayne State University and, in 1973, received a doctorate in sociology of education from Michigan State University. Ron has taught at all educational levels, including elementary, junior and senior high, junior college, and college. He was also a professor of sociology at the University of Florida. Later, he became a government research manager for the National Institute of Education and the US Commission on Civil Rights.

Among his many accomplishments, Ron was the first Black research director and longest-serving department director at the National Education Association, serving for a total of twenty-nine years at NEA and retiring in 2012. Highlights of his career include publishing thirty scholarly articles; serving as editor or co-editor of three academic books; making fifty three presentations at professional meetings; and serving as research manager at two government agencies, board member of the Horowitz Foundation, member of the Research Network, and chair of the Research Institute Board in Brussels, Belgium. Ron is a founding member of the board of the Bill Anderson Fund, an effort to expand the number of minority professionals in the field of disease and hazard research and practice.

Since 1989, he and wife Inez Thornton Henderson have made their home in Maryland.

- Rahman Henderson (October 4, 1976), son of Ron and Grace Gist Henderson, was an outstanding high school student who was the overall winner of his high school's science fair in 1994. After graduation, he attended the University of Maryland Baltimore County (UMBC) on a science and technology Meyerhoff scholarship. Dr. Freeman H. Hrabowski III, president of UMBC, told Rahman's parents that their son would have been awarded a scholarship on his application alone but that winning the science fair at Eleanor Roosevelt High School was a top-notch achievement. After graduating as a McNair Scholar with a major in math and minor in statistics, Rahman was awarded a full scholarship to the School of Engineering at the University of Wisconsin at Madison. He graduated in 2000 with a degree in industrial engineering and has worked at Southwest Airlines and General Electric in medical and business areas.

Currently, he is employed with United Airlines as the director of customer service and employee advocacy. Prior to this, he served as a manager of continuous improvement at O'Hare Airport in Chicago. One item on his bucket list is to visit every continent in the world.

He is married to Davina Sparks Henderson, a sales representative for Seattle Genetics.

Bernard (Ben) Henderson earned his bachelor's from St. Mary's College, a master of arts in organization management, and an MBA from the University of Phoenix. He has worked for Pacific Gas and Electric, as the manager of an AT&T mobile phone center, and as an instructor of business administration and organization at the University of Phoenix. After serving in the US Navy, Bernard settled in California with wife Exie Louise Bush, who passed away on September 28, 2007. He is currently married to Nancy Gilliam Henderson.

- Tanya Denise Henderson has a bachelor of science degree in nursing from the University of Phoenix and a master's in nursing from the University of San Francisco. She is married to Rodney Fryer, and they have four children.

- Shai'la Fryer graduated from the University of California, Santa Barbara with a degree in sociology and Black studies. Since 2014, she has been employed at Pacific Gas and Electric while exploring several entrepreneurial endeavors. She once lived and worked in China, but now resides in LA, working in the entertainment industry.

- Sah'Neya Fryer served four years in the US Navy and was honorably discharged in 2017. She is a presently a student at the University of California, East Bay.

- Rodney Fryer Jr. attended Modesto Junior College; he is now employed at Pacific Gas and Electric.

- Syd'Nee Fryer is attending Southern Oregon University on a basketball scholarship.

- Tami Henderson is an administrative assistant at Alco Iron and Metal.

Frankie DeVonne Henderson has a Bachelor of Science degree in criminal justice from Wayne State University. Over the years, she worked for Michigan Bell Telephone Company, for the Detroit Police Department, as the first Black undercover racetrack investigator, and as an unemployment fraud investigator for the State of Michigan. Frankie has also worked at Home Depot and with H&R Block as a tax preparer. She has one daughter.

- Mary Turnley graduated from Eastern Michigan University with a bachelor's degree and is currently enrolled in the MBA program. Multitalented and creative, Mary has established an event-planning consulting service called 2Entertain U, LLC. She has also performed in a live comedy play called "Call Waitin'" and was a member of a comedic team with JHines Comedy. She is currently employed with North American Bankcard

Michael T. Kirkland completed high school in Highland Park, Michigan, and joined the US Army, from which he was honorably discharged. He is employed as a school paraprofessional. A professional bass guitarist, Mike plays with several musical groups in the San Francisco Bay Area and has multiple solo albums on iTunes.

He and Spring Daughtry are the parents of one daughter, Leiyah Kirkland.

Kenneth Kirkland completed high school in Highland Park and later worked for Pacific Gas & Electric. He is the father of four: Kendell, Kanica, Kenneth, Jr., and Kimberly.

- Kendell Kirkland, who resides in Southfield, Michigan, has earned a Bachelor of Science degree in civil engineering, a Master's of Business Administration (MBA) and a master's of public administration from the University of Phoenix. Kendell has held several administrative positions with Blue Cross/Blue Shield of Michigan: as manager of health plan administration, manager of health plan business compliance and project support and as senior sales analyst. At one time, she also worked at DaimlerChrysler Corporation, Chrysler Financial Services. She and husband Angelo Murphy, Sr., are the parents of Angelo Murphy, Jr.

Derrick Lionell Pauling and Armari Darzell Murphy.

- Kanica Kirkland

- Kenneth Kirkland, II, and wife Paisley Shaw have one daughter, Jordyn Kirkland.

- Kimberly Kirkland

Arthuretta (Retta or Sugar Pie) Kirkland married Jimmy Oliver Zeigler, who served in the US Air Force, and they settled in Maryland to raise their three sons: Jimmy, Jeffrey, and Jason.

Retta earned a bachelor's in nursing from Bowie State University in Maryland and a master's in health-care administration from Central Michigan University. She also earned a master's in nursing from the University of Phoenix. Retta has held several supervisory positions and served as the dean of nursing in hospitals in the District of Columbia-Maryland-Virginia region. She is now on the nursing staff of a charter school in Washington, DC.

- Jimmy Oliver Zeigler Jr. has worked in residential and corporate real estate for more than a decade. He attended the University of Virginia, where he met his wife Elisa Larsen of Minnesota; they are the parents of Owen Christopher, Ella Marie, and Abigail Lynn.

- Jeffrey Owen Zeigler attended Howard University and married Vacinia Perry, with whom he had three children: Jason Oliver, Noah Elijah, and Tyler Reanne. He is currently married to Kenya Edens. Jeffrey is the owner of the Ultimate Source, an IT firm located in Bowie, Maryland. He holds many software certifications and licenses.

- Jason Omar Zeigler was an outstanding high school student who graduated as a National Merit Scholar and was awarded a full scholarship to the Honors College at the University of Oklahoma. He graduated from Oklahoma in three years, the only Black student in his Honors College graduating class with a dual degree in sociology and African-American studies.

Jason then received a scholarship to the New York University School of Law, from which he graduated with a superlative record. Highlights of his legal career include being listed as a Super Lawyer (2012–2017); receiving the E. Randolph Williams Award for public service *pro bono* (2005–2015); and being named counsel (2012–2015) and partner (2015–2017). In 2015, Jason founded RB5 Investments, which provides homes for homeless veterans. In 2017, he founded his own law firm—Zeigler Law, LLC.

He and wife Jana Brown Zeigler are the parents of son, Isaiah Cole, and daughter, Maya.

Elder Mary Helen (Tap) Kirkland is a licensed practice nurse (LPN) with a Bachelor of Science degree in nursing. She has practiced nursing in various medical facilities and organizations: Detroit Osteopathic Hospital, Detroit Riverview Hospital, Hospice of Michigan, and Blue Cross and Blue Shield. She is currently employed as a case manager with Molina Healthcare. Mary Helen and former husband Ricardo Thomas Sr. had three children:

- Ricardo Thomas Jr. is employed by the Amazon Fulfillment Center.

- Elder Tamara (Micki) Thomas holds three degrees from Eastern Michigan University (EMU): a bachelor's in elementary education, a master's in educational leadership and administration, and a specialist of arts degree in educational leadership. For more than twenty years, she taught school, served as a new teacher mentor/mentee, and was an administrator in Michigan's elementary and secondary schools. She was also an instructional coach for area consulting firms.

  Tamara was married to Courtney Lots; they are the parents of Kourtney and Kylee.

- Morris H. R. (Moe) Thomas, PhD, has earned multiple degrees from several leading universities: a PhD in higher education (administration) from Morgan State University (Baltimore, Maryland); an MA in educational policy and leadership from Ohio State University in Columbus, Ohio; an MS in instructional technology management from LaSalle University of Philadelphia, Pennsylvania; an MM in classical voice performance from New Jersey City University, Jersey City, New Jersey; and a BA in music (vocal performance) from Fisk University in Nashville, Tennessee; and he completed some postgraduate studies in project management at Cornell University and Georgetown University.

  Dr. Thomas serves as director for the Center

for the Advancement of Learning in the Learning Resources Division. He previously held positions in administration at several public, private, for-profit, and nonprofit institutions and organizations. He is an adjunct professor for the College of Agriculture, Urban Sustainability and Environmental Sciences, and has also taught for the College of Arts and Sciences at the University of the District of Columbia. Additionally, Moe has an active research agenda and has published in several refereed journals and other scholarly publications. He is the author of *Focus: The Missing Factor—A Practical Guide to Accomplishing Your Goals.*

In addition to academic pursuits, Dr. Thomas is a highly acclaimed opera singer who has performed with leading opera companies in the nation: Washington National Opera, Michigan Opera Theater, Opera San Jose, Amici Opera, New Jersey State Opera, Americolor Opera Alliance, Capitol City Opera, the Operantics, and West Bay Opera.

- Krystyn Thomas is married to Christian Speight; they have two daughters, Honesty and Hailee.

Melvin Kirkland (June 8, 1948–September 29, 1977) was a six-foot, four-inch, good-looking guy with a vibrant personality who lived life to the fullest. He was impressive as the drum major leading the Highland Park High School Marching Band. He was so impressive, in fact, that he was awarded a band scholarship to Grambling University in Louisiana.

Marvin Tilden Kirkland (October 2, 1960–November 24, 2000) was the youngest of the six Kirkland children raised in Highland Park. As a child, he attended Eastern Star Missionary Baptist Church and was baptized with his brother Michael. He later relocated to Maryland, where he graduated from Parkdale High School in Lanham. After graduation, he enlisted in the US Navy and received an honorable discharge. He was employed by the US Postal Service.

He and Della Maples are the parents of Marvin Tilden Kirkland Jr.

Ethel Ruby (Honey) Childs (February 28, 1922– December 28, 2006) was born in Ensley, Alabama, and attended the Rattan School of the Alabama School System. She accepted Christ as her  personal Savior and was baptized at the Woodlawn

Baptist Church. On January 17, 1937, she married Henry Starks of Montgomery, Alabama; the two relocated to Detroit, where they raised their ten children. Most of her work history was in private homes for prominent Detroit- area jeweler Sidney Krandall of Krandall and Sons Fine Jewelry and for the Lichterman family, who were involved in Cradle Pictures Inc. She lived a quiet life centered on God and her family. She loved cooking, gardening, attending plays, visiting her sons in California and Kentucky, and attending Ward family reunions when possible.

In 1949, Ethel Ruby became an active member of Greater Quinn AME Church, where she served as president of the altar guild, on the choir, and in any capacity called upon for fifty-seven years. During her home-going celebration in 2006, her children paid tribute in a statement called "Mother: God's Shining Light" (paraphrased here).

> Someone touched us not long ago, and her
> virtues are exemplified in women of the
> Bible. She was Deborah, judge of Israel,
> in that she led five generations of her

family with care, love, compassion, and wisdom. She was Esther, queen of Israel, in that the sweet fragrance of positivity, beauty, and stately meekness resounded wherever she went. She was Naomi, as she was loyal, trustworthy, and true. And last, she was Mary, the mother of Jesus, demonstrating stamina, strength, and resolve while enduring the deaths of four children. Yes, someone touched us not long ago. May her light forever shine— Ethel Ruby, family matriarch.

Henry Starks Jr. passed away when he was four years old.

Barbara Jean Starks (who, as of the writing of this Ward history, at eighty-one years old, is the oldest surviving member of the Starks family) studied at the Highland Park General School of Nursing and later transferred to the Detroit School of Nursing. After her marriage to John King and a series of adversities, she persevered with her studies and, in 1990, received her nursing degree eleven years later. Barbara Jean served as an intensive care, surgical, and neurological surgery nurse for sixteen years.

Lisa King had a stellar high school career at Cass Technical High School, finishing in the top 1 percent of her class. With scholarships from several sources that covered her school expenses, she then attended Hampton University and Michigan State University and graduated from the University of Detroit (now University of Detroit Mercy). Lisa's greatest impact as a student was at the University of Detroit Mercy when she sat as a student member of the board of directors, participated in the Black Student Organization sit-ins, and helped revise the student government structure, a structure which remains today. She graduated in 1994 and took a position at Ford Motor Credit Company.

Rebecca (Beck) Starks was trained as both a phlebotomist and a cosmetologist. As the former, Beck worked for years in the department of pathology at Henry Ford Hospital. However, most of her career was as a cosmetologist at Shep's Barber Shop for the barber who gave the Henderson, Kirkland, and Starks boys haircuts during their early years. While at Shep's, Beck provided cosmetic services to her mother, Ethel Ruby; Aunt Mary Ella; and many other family members for years.

Hurvie Mae Starks (May 24, 1943–July 15, 1989) was born in Detroit but raised in Highland Park. Early in life, she accepted Christ as her Savior and joined Greater Quinn AME Church.

She was active in Sunday school and directed the Celestials, a singing aggregation. Hurvie was described as loving, caring, sharing, and unselfish and as a valiant warrior.

After attending the public schools of Highland Park, she became one of the first Black students to attend the prestigious Interlochen Arts Music Camp, located in northern Michigan, on a cello scholarship and later sang with Harold Smith and the Majestics. Hurvie later matriculated at Highland Park Community College.

Our family is eternally grateful to Hurvie for organizing the first Ward/Childs family reunion forty years ago. In the booklet she wrote during the 1970s, she recalled visiting the ancestral homestead in Browns, Alabama, with cousin Ed Ward, great-grandson of Matt and Ella:

Ed and I drove off the highway onto an old dusty dirt road and at the base of that road was a majestic, magnificent and mighty oak tree. It was the most beautiful tree I had ever seen standing there in all her splendor, totally untouched by the pollution and chemical spoils of our northern way of life. As I stood under that magnificent oak, I thought of Matt and Ella and of the countless times they possibly had travelled that old dusty dirt road. In utter silence with a gentle breeze blowing peacefully across the Ward family's 500 acre-soybean field, I closed my eyes and could envision my great grandparents welcoming me, reaching out saying, "We're so glad you came."

Lee Franklin Starks (September 16, 1944–August 24, 1981) was born in Detroit to Ethel Ruby Childs and Henry Starks. Early in life, he united with and was baptized at the family church and sang on the Sunbeam choir. He grew up in Highland Park, where he attended public schools, graduating from Highland Park High School in 1962. He was an outstanding tackle on the football team, a member of the Letterman's club, and a drummer in the school band.

Lee was a friendly and outgoing person with a big smile and a heart of gold, always placing others before himself.

Theodore Starks attended Northern Arizona University on a basketball scholarship, later earning his Bachelor of Science degree. He enlisted in the US Army in 1967, enjoying a stellar career, and graduated from military intelligence, jump school, Ranger training, and special forces. He was promoted to E-5 Sergeant (NCO) and then to Warrant Officer Second Class. In 1975, Theodore was named Outstanding Young Man of America.

After his military service, Theodore began a career as a wine and spirits salesman and later as marketing manager and district marketing analyst with Standard Oil of Michigan and Indiana. His final post before retiring was as president of Third World Developers Inc., a company that involved the worldwide import and export of oil.

Sylvester Starks (July 24, 1946–October 23, 2004) was the sixth of the ten Starks children. Along with other members of his family, he joined the Greater Quinn AME Church, attended Sunday school, sang in the Sunbeam and Celestial choirs, and served as co-chairman of the annual Men's Day celebration at the church. Affectionately known as Midnight Sparrow, Sylvester was employed by the Chrysler Corporation for several years and later with Lear Seating Corporation until coming down with an illness in February 2004.

He began working at twelve years old and was a hard worker, taking on different jobs to help support his family. Sylvester was a loving father to his ten children with Bettina Brooks and with Patricia Seabrooks, whom he married on August 15, 1964.

- Darius (Buddha) Brooks and three children: Nikia (Nikki), Lawrence, and Daniel Brooks

- Robert Brooks and three children: Carlton Gipson, Robert Jr., and Henry Brooks

- Sylvester Troy and daughter Ryan

- Elesa Starks and LaVerne White and children: Carlos, Camille, LaTonya, and LaToya

- Kimberly Starks and husband Dwight, son Donte

- Henry Starks Jr. and wife Karen and three children: Henry Jr., Jonathan, and Lexis

- Marcus Starks is the father of one, Marquetta, and grandfather of five: Kamari, Yonna, Ziya, Kennedy, and Angel

- Mesha Starks and children: Jazmine and Janice

- Michael Starks and children: Semaje, Zehaya, Gianna, and Michael Jr.

- Dawn Starks and children: D'John, Johnell, Ashley, and Alexis

Evonne (Tommie) Starks (November 14, 1949–July 22, 2016) attended area public schools and the Community College of Highland Park. She was both athletic and musical, earning letters in swimming and tennis and a full, four-year scholarship to the Interlochen Arts Music Camp. An accomplished cellist with the Highland Park Orchestra, she was later accepted to The Juilliard School in New York City.

Tommie was employed by the Chrysler Corporation when she was involved in a major car accident that resulted in the loss of a leg.

Sharon Starks attended Highland Park Public Schools and has been a homemaker and caregiver, certified as a nurse's assistant in Michigan. She is married to Lawrence Willoughby; they are the parents of Andre Bascom and Lawanda Willoughby.

Carl Starks is a graduate of Control Data Institute with certification in programming. For thirty-three years, he has been an information systems specialist, holding positions at American Fletcher National Bank (AFNB) and Pacific Gas and Electric Management Information Systems International (including positions with their subsidiaries Comerica Bank and Volkswagen America), Henry Ford Health Systems, and Apex/ Bank of America in Richmond, Virginia. Carl is currently employed with Humana.

He and his wife Valicia Robinson Starks have three children and two grandchildren.

- Cortez Starks graduated from Michigan State University with a Bachelor of Science degree in interdisciplinary studies in economics. During college, he was a page in the Michigan House of Representatives and an intern with State Farm. He has held professional positions with Enterprise Rentals, Chase Bank, and Fidelity Brokerage as a certified financial planner.

He is married to Tiana Starks; they are the parents of Kinedy and Terrell.

- Terrell Starks (May 21, 1986–May 24, 2010)

- Dominique Starks (December 16, 1987–March 14, 2005)

CHAPTER 15
WE ARE WARD PROUD

After putting pen to paper (or, in the language of the times, stylus to screen), the authors of this book are pleased to have moved our family's narrative from oral to documented history so that future generations will know their roots without equivocation. The lessons we have learned since starting this project have solidified our own knowledge as we uncovered new facts; shared details with family members; read voluminous interview guides; and heard stories via phone, emails, texts, and social media about our ancestors and their descendants.

To create as complete and accurate a history as possible, we also meticulously searched the archives in Alabama and US Census data for documents about births and deaths, and, to our amazement, we located the official marriage license of Madison Matt Ward and Ella Duncan (spelled *Dunkin*). This discovery not only sealed for us the legitimacy of their union, but it also revealed the names of another generation of Wards and Duncans, the names of the fathers of the engaged couple—Alonzo Ward and William Dunkin—since they had to witness for their children with the infamous "X."

This historical document is not necessarily the result of our many accomplishments, since many of our ancestors failed and perhaps could be said to have lived despicable lives. But it is because of the favor of God all over this family and our determination to remain faithful to His Word, His will, and His way. By the grace of Almighty God, He placed something in the DNA of Matt and Ella Ward nearly two hundred years ago that has passed from generation to generation to remind each of us that *we are somebody in His sight* and *we bow down to no man*. In the words of Jeremiah 1:5, which speaks of a personal, intimate relationship with God, "Before I formed thee in the womb I knew you; and before thou camest forth out of the womb I sanctified [consecrated] thee."

For the Wards, it is not familial arrogance or personal perfection but an awareness that God knows our name; He knew us before the foundation of the world and had anointed and appointed the former slave and his wife to raise up children in the admonition of God, to worship Him, to serve Him, to serve the church and the wider community, and to make each corner brighter because a Ward family member passed by.

Since January 2017, we have become profoundly aware of the *oneness* of our family, who remains committed to the well-being of each generation and to the continued success of Ward family reunions. In the twenty-first century, these bi-annual events are tantamount to the annual pilgrimages "to the country" a long time ago, to Browns and Uniontown, Alabama, each summer to reconnect with family and to spend time with Grandma Ella and the many, many siblings, cousins, aunts, uncles, nieces, and nephews.

Our prayer is that *We Are the Wards!* will knit the Ward family even closer and closer still in the *Oneness* of God the Father, God the Son, and God the Holy Spirit.

Amen.

APPENDIX

WE ARE THE WARDS

(The Ward family anthem sung to the
tune of "We Are the World")
by Rev. Gloria Ward Wyatt

We are the Wards; we're true descendants
We've come from far and near to here; so let's start
loving.

Chorus
It's a choice we're making
We're spreading unity
So we stand to say "hoo-ray" for the Ward family.

We are the Wards; we are their children
We wish you love and peace and joy; so let's not
waste it.

Chorus

And so to Matt and Ella
We sing this tribute song
For without the love of them
We wouldn't be here.

We are the Wards; we're true descendants
We've come from far and near to here; so let's start
loving.

Chorus

APPENDIX
THAT OLD DUSTY DIRT ROAD

CHAPTER I

It has taken much work to put "REUNION 1979" together. I began working on this year's reunion last year in August, just two short weeks after the closing of "REUNION 1978". In putting "REUNION 1979" together- it ultimately carried me to the State of Alabama. Into Birmingham, from Birmingham to Ensley, from Ensley to Fairfield, from Fairfield, to Bessemer, from Bessemer, to Uniontown, and down into a tiny little city called Browns.

I was taken to Browns by Clark Edward Ward, Jr., one of the sons of Clark Edward Ward, Sr., better known to most of us as Jake. When I reached Browns, my first stop was at the home of William and Violet

Ward Cooke. Violet is the daughter of Odie and Carrie Jefferson Ward.

As I walked onto Violet's porch, I found myself thinking of this dear lady who has lived better than three quarters of a century and of how much she must surely have seen, and of how much wisdon must surely abound in her. Although she does not get around very well any more or see very well any more she is still a very vibrant senior.

I took a seat on the porch near Violet as she was stitching and putting together throw pillows. As we began to talk she dropped her needle to the porch and asked me if I would pick it up for her. When I picked up the needle, I threaded it for her and looking at her with a smile which she returned, I said --- "Bye, tell me what you know of the Ward Families." She turned, looking at me again with a smile and said "Well Hurvie Mae my memory doesn't serve me very well any more." But of those things that she could clearly remember, she remembered Grandma and Grandpa being meager farmers and starting out with only the tin top wooden shanty they owned and a mere acre of land.

Large families were profitable in the south and so

as Matt and Ella Duncan Ward's family grew, thus did the prosperity of the Wards.

CHAPTER II

Unfortunately, little accurate informational data could be gathered regarding the early lives of the Ward or Childs Families.

Our roots can however be traced back to the soil of the State of Alabama, one of the most notorious states in the deep South, not only in our ancestors time, but in our time as well.

I do know factually that our ancestors were born during the era of slavery and almost certainly during the early 1840's. The exact dates of birth are unknown.

As most blacks were, Matt and Ella Duncan Ward were probably born in old wooden shacks and probably with the bear earth serving as a floor. This would serve as their home. This was where they would be reared. Although, these homes were indeed humble, they were homes of deep religious belief in the Lord. I firmly believe that Matt and Ella Duncan Ward were reared in homes where Jesus was a much talked about subject.

They were perhaps often taken to their worshipping places where those of the slavery era would meet and sing songs such as: "Down By the Riverside," "Swing Low, Sweet Chariot," "Rock My Soul," and "Still Away to Jesus." It is also possible that the worshipping place was Woodlawn.

It is probably certain that they worked in the fields of Cotton as most did during that era and yet, Matt and Ella survived like many other of the deeply rooted South.

Can you visualize a small Black Girl or Boy growing up under those conditions? Can you actually picture them as they grew until finally they are approaching man and womanhood, and having great dreams and aspirations and looking forward to the day when oppression is NO MORE?

CHAPTER III

Envision Matt and Ella Duncan Ward as the Abraham's of this family. Envision them reading the words recorded in the book of GENESIS 17:20. "And as for Ishmael, I have heard thee: Behold, I have blessed him, and will make him fruitful, and will multiply him exceedingly; twelve princes shall he beget, and I will make him a great nation."

By this time the issue of slavery is being much discussed between the North and the South. While the issue of slavery is being addressed, I can imagine that Matt and Ella Duncan Ward are dreaming of a way to make it over. A way to the much Promised Land. Then, the end of the Civil War. Now come the reaping.

Some years have passed now and Matt and Ella come to the tiny town of Browns, Alabama with their families. As the family grows, thus does the prosperity of the Wards.

The meager acre of land has been purchased, a small Corn and Cotton crop is now planted, several milk cows and a bull are bought. The finishing touches of the mules, chickens and pigs are added, and the homesteading on the same spot of land occupied by Ward family members now is begun.

Matt and Ella have become inlaws as well as grandparents now. Odie Ward has married Carrie Jefferson who bears five children. James Golden Ward has married Eugenia Mason who bears three children. William Ward has married Chaney Fields, who bears three children, Ludie Ward has married Rebecca (Maiden name unknown), who bears three children, Laura Ward marries Herbert Childs and they have two daughters, and Isabelle Ward marries (name could not be located) and they have one daughter.

CHAPTER IV

After chatting with Bye (Violet) for nearly three hours, eating home made Biscuits which Bessie had come down from Georgia and made, and that good ole Southern Sausage along with home made preserves, I got into one of the cars and went down the road a piece to Ed's house and chatted with Bernice his wife and Tommie and Ed his sons. From there I went down to Blanche's trailer, on down to John and Annie Mae's and then finally down to Minnie and Lee's. The conversation was pretty much the same in all of the stops that I had made in that little tiny town of Browns, what information could I gather with regard to my people.

When I returned to Ed's house late that evening around the time of what they refer to as "First Dark," he and I along with Lee got into one of the cars and went to dinner. We spent a great part of the evening talking about the state of affairs of the world and how deeply peaceful it must have seemed during Matt and Ella's time while they must surely have been very deeply burdened during that era. After we had conversed for several hours we started home. Lee was the first to reach home and when we had let him out of the car we were going down the highway back to Ed's when suddenly I glanced out across a huge field. Not realizing then that this too was family property I said to Ed, "What is that spot?" He turned to look at me with a smile and asked me if I remembered this location since it had been nearly twenty-five years since I was last down there. My reply was, "Isn't this where the compound of Ward homes stood?" Looking rather dazed by my remarks Ed replied yes, but how could you remember that? Somehow, I could not explain how I recognized this area but there was something so very familiar about it and I said "I must go down there."

We drove down off of the highway onto an old dusty

dirt road and at the base of that road was a majestic, magnificent, and mighty Oak Tree. I suspect that it must be about the most beautiful tree that I have ever seen standing there in all her splendor totally untouched by the pollution and chemical spoils of our northern way of life. As I stood there under that magnificent Oak Tree many, many thoughts ran through my mind. I thought of Matt and Ella Duncan Ward and of the countless times they had travelled that road and how that old Oak Tree had seen the footsteps that were taken on that old dirt road. While standing there in utter silence for a long period with a gentle breeze blowing so peacefully across that 500 acre Soybean field and blowing ever so gently in my hair I but closed my eyes and it was as though I could see Matt and Ella Duncan Ward. When the silence had finally broken I said: "You know Ed, this reminds me of something that was said once by an old slaveperson about an Oak Tree, and as I stand here I find that I too wonder if this old Oak hasn't seen more than I'll ever see; doesn't know more than I'll ever know and if she hasn't heard more than I'll ever hear and if she could but talk to us what stories she would certainly be able to tell." Then,

I began stepping out onto that old dusty dirt road and with each step I took is was as if I was being welcomed by my ancestors. It was as if I could so clearly see Matt and Ella Duncan Ward and it seemed that they might reach out and touch upon me and speak to me saying "We're so very glad you came." When I turned going back up that road toward that ole' mighty Oak Tree I realized that I had to put this into writing. I realized that I had to try to express to each of you some of the experiences I had found in that little tiny city called Browns and I realized that I would call it: "That Old Dusty Dirt Road," because there is no other known passage way down into that vast acreage but by way of "That Old Dusty Dirt Road." I thought of what Matt and Ella had gone through coming up in the era of slavery and I thought of what they had gone through to insure that this would be a landmark of the Wards families and of what they had gone through to insure that their offsprings would have a better way of life.

I thought of what our ancestors had gone through to insure that this property would remain in the control of the Wards. Then, I began to think of the vast and marvelous contribution Matt and Ella Duncan

Ward had made to this country in the forms of their children, in the forms of men and women and how deeply respected they were throughout the state and what a proud, stern people they were. I thought of the contribution made to the medical profession, to the field of chemistry and physics, and the educational profession, and to the business world and of the writers and finally of the two daughters of Herbert and Laura Ward Childs who would both simultaneously in the year 1976 be bestowed one of the highest honors that can be placed upon a mother in this country - their two sons election and induction into the "OUTSTANDING YOUNGMEN OF AMERICA" for the year 1976. And then, I thought of all of the other wonderful contributions made by the offsprings of Matt and Ella Duncan Ward- Spiritually, Culturally, Educationally. I thought of how tremendously far we had come as an individual family body from the days of grave oppression to "REUNION 1979."

I thought of how far we had come down "THAT OLD DUSTY DIRT ROAD."

My dear family, my loved ones, I am sure that if Matt and Ella Duncan were with us today that he would stand in the proud, stern manner known to the Ward men and say "Chillun, you do me proud." And I suspect that if Ella could take her place along side her husband she would say in that manner so commonly known to her "Chillun, you do me proud."

We have travelled across the roads of Slavery, up the roads of Reconstruction, and down "THAT OLD DUSTY DIRT ROAD."

We have much to be proud of. We are of Ward/Childs Stock.

CROSS-WARD PUZZLE

Created by Rev. Jaki Hall

ACROSS

1,2,4	Every 2 yrs.
8	Honey's older daughter
9	Hits the_____
13	Ancestral_____(s)
15	Interrogative pronoun
16	Lucie Cooke-Dawson
18	Ward family crop
20	It keeps us together
22	Two cousins' names combined
24	The original family crop
26	Site of the 2000 reunion
27	Reunion event
28	Arlene's older daughter
29	"___ Are the Wards!"
30	Ernestine Shepperd's nickname
31	Synonym for family
32	Ethel Childs Starks
34	Ed's oldest son (dec.)
39	Honey's oldest son
41	Ella's maiden name
42	Short for Brother
43	Abbrev. for compact disk
44	Another of Ed's sons
46	A Violet Ridgeway (nickname)
47	Mary Ella's son
49	To get the gray out
50	Ala. university & city
53	Not the front
54	Another reunion event
55	Violet Cooke's nickname
56, 57, 58	We celebrate their _____

DOWN

1	Site of the 2004 reunion
2	We always have so much___
3	2nd site of the 2004 reunion
4	Ralph Ward's monogram
5	Ancestral hometown
6, 33	2004 reunion motto
7	_____ Ward-Davis
10	Otis Ward as grandfather
11	Opposite of off
12	Thomas Jefferson Ward (dec.)
14	"The ____that Binds"
17	One of the longest living matriarchs
19	Dorothy Ward Reeves
21	Sister's real name
23	In English, an article
24	All Ward babies are _____
25	A mineral or a rock
35	Clark Edward Ward, Jr.'s nickname
36	Myrt's formal name
37	One of Matt & Ella's sons
38	The Wards' original occupation
39	Something borrowed
40	_____ Ward-Shears
45	Another of the oldest living matriarchs
48	Another of Matt & Ella's sons
51	Hardie ____ Ward (dec.)
52	Mildred Cooke Miree

Printed in the United States
By Bookmasters